CITIZENS OF LONG AGO

THE EMPEROR JULIAN, *See page* 146

CITIZENS OF LONG AGO

ESSAYS ON LIFE AND LETTERS IN THE ROMAN EMPIRE

BY

ADELINE BELLE HAWES
LATE PROFESSOR EMERITUS OF LATIN
IN WELLESLEY COLLEGE

Essay Index Reprint Series

BOOKS FOR LIBRARIES PRESS, INC.
FREEPORT, NEW YORK

First published 1934
Reprinted 1967

PRINTED IN THE UNITED STATES OF AMERICA

CONTENTS

INTRODUCTION

ADELINE BELLE HAWES

(May 26, 1857 — November 14, 1932)

READERS who value the classical humanities will very much like these final essays of Adeline Belle Hawes. Seven of the nine are concerned with personalities of the ancient Roman world attractive either in themselves or their associations. In " Light Reading from the Roman Empire," the immortal *Golden Ass* of Apuleius is hardly more entertaining than the character and fortunes of its quick-witted and adventurous author himself. Fronto, the " Friend of Marcus Aurelius," will always command our interest because of his nearness to the most appealing of emperors. Rutilius Namatianus, " A Roman Poet of the Fifth Century," is an eloquent voice in appreciation of Rome the Mother at a time when the temporal powers of the Eternal City were already far on in their transformation to the spiritual. " The Emperor Julian " is made better known to us as the lover of letters, the mover in reform, and the victim of misjudgment as Julian the Apostate. In " A Greek Satirist of the Roman Empire," we meet again Lucian of Samosata, whose sharp vision of what is behind the tattered mask of humanity has given the world some of its most famous drolleries. The human biographer of the most human of the Greeks and Romans receives his due in " Plutarch in his Essays " where he is presented to us as the delightfully gracious and kindly old gentleman who has travelled much, who has known " beautiful Rome," but who has never thought of making a home elsewhere than in his dull native Chaeronea, the " town already so small that he could not bear to make it smaller by the loss of a single citizen." In " A Spanish Poet in Rome," we learn to know better the quick-eyed and keen-witted Martial, the stuff of whose epigrams is the variegated humanity of the great capital. If the two remaining essays do not so distinctly center about single figures, " Little Citizens of Long Ago " and " Charities and Philanthropies in the Roman Empire " are still of the deepest human interest in their appeal to our love of children and our appreciation of generous motives.

Not only in matter, but in method, style, and spirit, are Miss Hawes's essays what is expected of the mature classicist. There is in them no dull exhaustiveness, no forced arrangement, no torturing of evidence, none of the pomposity of " contribution." She chooses from abundant material what is important to the clothing of her figures with character, and does not burden her page with the superfluous or the irrelevant. Her presentations follow no formula, but are the natural and easy exposition of one on familiar terms with her evidence. Their unpretentious style is appropriate to her purpose of bringing within reach of modern humanity these living figures of a remote but real and related past. The result of her effort is something ripe and mellow which ingratiates her subjects with the general reader, and which veterans of the classics themselves may read with edification.

The humanist reader will find appropriate the manner in which these essays came into being. Miss Hawes retired from the Wellesley Faculty in 1925, after an active and distinguished service of thirty-seven years. For more than twenty-five years she had spent summers and sabbatical years in Rome, so that upon retirement as *Emerita* it was quite natural for her to turn her steps toward Rome. She made her home on the Esquiline, in the distinguished household affectionately known to so many classical humanists. There she met in pleasant association old friends and new, until late in the autumn of 1932 she was called to join the numerous company of those from her own land who

" Have sunk to rest in the arms of Rome."

During the seven years of her Roman residence she was in the spiritual sense a citizen of Rome, Rome both modern and ancient, Eternal Rome. She spoke its language, thought its thoughts, rejoiced in its successes, partook of its ambitions, shared its pride. She enjoyed with keen and undiminished interest the wealth of opportunities afforded by the world's most attractive and inspiring city, the city which had so long been the center of her instruction and her thoughts, the city of her soul. She delighted in its natural beauties — its newly created and its age-old gardens, the wonders of May and the flowers, golden October and full-clustered autumn, the geniality of June sunlight, the soft freshness of summer mornings and the reposeful cool of summer evenings, the colorful displays of Christmas and Eas .er, the rich hues of Roman sunsets. George Meason Whicher's lines in " The Spanish Steps " are almost as eloquent for the Esquiline with *its* " cataract stairs ":

> " On either side the houses stand
> Orange-russet, buff, and tanned;
> With the cataract stairs aflow from above
> In the dead-leaf tints that painters love. . . .
> And bent over all the wondrous hue
> Of a Roman winter's tender blue."

Amid these scenes and in these enjoyments, which were sometimes dulled but never destroyed by the pangs of increasing ailment, Miss Hawes did not cease to participate in the life of scholarly endeavor. She read and excerpted and wrote. She was a familiar figure in the library of the American Academy, and her name was generously on the roll of its supporters. She attended lectures and concerts, and frequented the sessions of learned societies, on occasion reading papers before them. She contributed to classical journals. She collected and set in order the matter of her essays. In their solidity of content, in their straightforward and unassertive manner, in their appreciation of the human motive, and now and then in their gleam of the personal, they are an example of classical humanism bearing fruit in the fulness of time and in the ideal place, and they form an appropriate memorial of their author's career and character.

GRANT SHOWERMAN

MADISON, WISCONSIN
June, 1934

LITTLE CITIZENS OF LONG AGO

An Italian characteristic, often remarked upon by Americans who are travelling in Italy, is a noticeable fondness for children. " How the Italians do love children! " is an exclamation that one often hears. But it is not of Italians of modern times only that this is characteristic. Anyone who once begins to notice the frequent and affectionate references to children in Latin literature, will be inclined to exclaim, " How the Romans did love children! " Even the title of this paper, " Little Citizens," is borrowed from a Roman author. Since devotion to the family, the love of home and all that home implies, was a characteristic of the Roman people, it was natural that frequent expression of the home instinct, frequent reference to the children of the home, should appear in the Roman writers. Yet the references to children in Roman literature are for the most part casual only. No Latin author ever wrote a treatise on the child life of his time. The Latin authors do not discuss child psychology or make childhood a special theme. But there are in Latin authors innumerable little touches which give glimpses, and in some cases present charming pictures, of healthy, happy childhood. These touches are for the most part very slight, but although the words are few, they often suggest far more than is expressed, and show, not only tender affection for some individual child, but also a keen appreciation of how a child feels, an understanding of the ways and the moods of childhood. The Romans did not idealize the child. They loved him and enjoyed him for just what he was, and however much the ways and customs of grown-ups may differ in different ages, the children of all times are very much the same.

Although the references to children in Latin literature are so numerous, nothing like a classification will be attempted, but the starting point may well be with the babies, since it was with two babies that Roman history began, and since very young babies appear in Roman literature. The first to be noticed is that verse in the famous Fourth Eclogue of Vergil,

Incipe, parve puer, risu cognoscere matrem.
(Begin, little one, to recognize mother with a smile.)

Vergil was not a father himself, but this verse shows that he had often watched little babies and noticed those faint, quick-vanishing smiles which come so early on a baby's face and by which the little one so soon begins to show that he knows his mother.

That baby who appears in the Aeneid is well known too, the little Camilla whose story no one who has once read could ever forget. We see her first an infant carried in her father's arms when fleeing from foes in hot pursuit he comes to a river swollen by recent storms. The only possible chance to escape is to swim to the other side. But the father fears for his precious burden, *caro oneri timet.* He dares not take the baby into those cold, rushing waters, and with hardly time to think what he is doing, without time enough to hesitate over the rashness of his deed, he binds her to a spear and, with a word of prayer, he hurls it. " Loud roared the waters and over the rushing river she sped, poor little Camilla, on a whizzing spear." The rest of the story is very charming, the description of the baby living alone with her father on the solitary hills, most tenderly cared for and taught to use the lance and the bow as soon as she could stand on her own little feet.

Another poet of the Augustan Age, Tibullus, refers very briefly in one passage to the old grandfather who is never tired of taking care of his baby grandson and amusing him with prattling baby-talk. Tibullus in very few words draws a picture which we may see repeatedly on the streets in any Italian town, the old man with the baby in his arms. Catullus too has occasional references to children as when he alludes, simply by way of comparison, to a little two-year-old " sleeping in the cradle of his father's tired arms," tired, but never too tired to hold the baby. In another poem Catullus pictures a common domestic scene when he refers to " little Torquatus in his mother's lap sweetly smiling and reaching out his baby hands to father." Long before the Madonna with her child were represented in Italian art, this sight of a mother holding her baby had delighted the Italian eye. Neither Catullus nor Tibullus had children of their own, but like all Italians they loved babies. The words, " reaching out his baby hands to father," recalls a passage in Quintilian. This is in the preface to the

sixth book where Quintilian gives his readers just a glimpse into
the love and the grief of his own home life and in referring to the
two little sons he had lost, his only children, he says with such a
note of affectionate pride that the baby would always leave anyone else to go to his father. Quintilian's love of children and his
understanding of them are abundantly illustrated in the first book
of his great work.

In the correspondence of Marcus Aurelius there are many references to his children when they were little. Fronto, the intimate friend of Marcus Aurelius, once went to see two of these
infants when their father was away from home and wrote him a
long letter about them. He assures the father that the babies had
excellent color and good strong lungs, *clamore forti,* and then adds,
" One of them was holding a piece of white bread like the son of
an Emperor, while the other had dark bread, as befits the son of a
philosopher." These two children were twins. One died at the
age of four years, while the other grew up to succeed his father
as Emperor. His reputation was such that it may be said that the
" Five Good Emperors," whose successive reigns covered a period
of nearly a hundred years, were followed by a man about as bad
as could be imagined. But which of the two had the white bread
and which ate the dark, history has never told. Fronto in this
letter refers to the children as " chicks," and Marcus Aurelius himself uses the same word in a letter to Fronto, saying, " Every chick
in our little nest begins to pray for you as soon as he is old
enough." Of a baby daughter of Marcus Aurelius when she was
about six months old Fronto writes, " She is such a serious, old-
fashioned little lady ! When I ask for her tiny hands or her plump
little feet to kiss, she draws them away or gives them grudgingly."
Anyone who is acquainted with babies can see her doing it. One
commentator on Fronto's letters uses the expression, " Greet your
children," as an argument for determining the date of a letter,
saying that in the year to which the letter has been ascribed the
children were too young to have a message sent them. But are
children ever too young to have a message sent them by their
grandfather or their father's intimate friend? Not if the writer
of the letter is a Roman. There is extant also a letter of Fronto
about his own little grandson. This baby was always saying,
" Give, Give," and when he said " Give," grandfather always gave

him something. American parents do not always realize when the baby says " Da, Da," that the precocious infant is talking Latin. Fronto often gave this baby pieces of writing paper to play with because he wanted him to become an author, but whether this early use of writing paper had the desired result or not, we can never know. The proud grandfather gravely states the fact that the baby enjoyed birds and chickens and puppies as if that were something distinctive, instead of being like all other babies. He is sure that this characteristic must have been inherited from himself, for he had been told by those who took care of him in his infancy that he too had enjoyed birds and chickens and puppies. Fronto was a genuine grandfather and therefore he was convinced that this little grandson of his was the most remarkable child that ever lived.

The reference to the babyhood of the Emperor Commodus in Fronto's letter to Marcus Aurelius recalls an anecdote of the Emperor Tiberius when he was a baby and on one occasion almost brought disaster on the family. The story is too long to relate but the gist of it is that in a time of danger, at a very critical moment when absolute silence was imperative, a man who, as the infant thought, had not been properly introduced, tried to take him from his mother's arms. Thereupon that young person did what any self-respecting baby would have done under the circumstances. He lifted up his voice in loud remonstrance, and in so doing he came near changing the course of Roman history.

It is well known that the Emperor Gaius when a little child was a great pet with the soldiers in his father's army. He was called the *alumnus legionum,* and about as soon as he could walk his mother dressed him in a little military costume including the high boots. The delighted soldiers used to call the kiddie " Little Boots " and this pet name has always clung to him. All through the ages he has been better known by the nickname Caligula than by his real name, although it is said that he himself much disliked it.

Of Augustus, while little is known in regard to his own childhood, it is interesting to learn that after he became Emperor, his favorite relaxation was either fishing or playing marbles with very small children.

No Roman so far as we know ever made a list of the first hundred words that a child spoke and philosophized upon them, but references to the child's first attempts at speech are not lacking. Lucretius has a pretty name for baby-talk, *infracta loquella*, and Tibullus speaks of it as *balba verba*. Statius says of a baby who is trying to talk that his lips are "wrestling" with words which his mind already thinks, and Minucius Felix refers to the charm of those half-formed words, the *dimidiata verba*, when a baby is just beginning to use words. The baby name for mother, as in many languages, was *mamma*, but instead of papa, the word *tata* was common, as babbo is in modern Italy, and in the south *tata* may still be heard.

There is a short passage in Vergil's Aeneid which illustrates a characteristic feature of Roman family life. Not many people perhaps remember that the old town of Gaeta on the coast between Naples and Rome was named, according to tradition, for the old nurse of Aeneas who died in the place where a town afterwards grew up. Four verses in the Aeneid tell of the death of Gaeta and the naming of the town in her honor, and that is all. That his old nurse should have gone with Aeneas in all his long wandering and stayed with him until she died, that she would not have been one of "the weak and the weary, and those who fearful of toil were left behind," all that is taken for granted. The introduction of this incident in the Aeneid has sometimes been criticized as being forced and unnatural, but the critics who say that have evidently never learned how sacred was the tie that bound the children's nurse to the Roman family. To the Roman readers of the Aeneid this reference to the nurse of Aeneas must have seemed perfectly natural, for it was out of existing customs that the legend grew. Many a tomb inscription of the Roman Empire might be cited to illustrate the legend. There is one in North Africa for instance on a tomb erected by an officer of the twenty-second legion to his old nurse who had died at the age of a hundred years. Of another old nurse who died somewhere in central Italy the one who erected the tomb says, "she followed us over sea and land all the way from Libyan shores." The nurse of the younger Pliny, to whom he gave a little farm in her old age, will be remembered by anyone familiar with his letters. Among the large number of nurses whose epitaphs are extant we find two who cared for the children of Germanicus, and another of rather special interest is the nurse of the great-grandchildren of Vespasian. Of her we learn from a broken inscription now in the Vatican. The mother of the children was the grand-daughter of Vespasian, and it was two of these grand-nephews whom Domitian had intended to appoint as his own successors. We remember also that it was the two old nurses of Nero who, faithful to the last, cared for his body and placed the urn containing his ashes in the family tomb. Many references to nurses are found also in the tomb inscriptions of little children, and among these inscriptions some of the sweetest and most pathetic are those expressing the love and grief of nurses whose little charges had died.

In the Aeneid the development of Ascanius is of much interest, although the references to him are so slight that it would be possible to read the Aeneid without really thinking much about this development. Ascanius was not old enough to be an important character in the story, but we have occasional glimpses of him, and every time he appears he has grown and developed since the time before. We see him first, that little tot clinging to his father's hand and trotting after him with his short baby steps, *non passibus aequis*. In Carthage the little boy was not too old to sit on Dido's lap, but old enough to be taken on the hunting expedition to his great joy, and when the older people were quite satisfied with the wild goats and stags as game, little Ascanius was praying for a " foaming boar or a tawny lion." Later on we see him a valiant little horseman when he leads the company of boys at the games in Sicily, and we remember how still later he chuckled at their " eating the tables " which he thought was such a joke. Thus we have one brief glimpse after another of Ascanius until the day when he shows himself such a manly boy in that beautiful scene with Nisus and Euryalus just before they start on their fatal quest. Warde Fowler had a theory that Vergil intended to portray in this scene how a noble Roman boy might conduct himself, if suddenly and long before he was old enough, he should be called upon to take his father's place. Ascanius rises to the occasion. He is very dignified, but even in his dignity he is a genuine boy, and some of the promises which he makes are as delightfully boyish as they are absurdly impossible.

Propertius is about the last poet of whom one would expect any reference to children. While much of the work of Propertius is very brilliant, yet his excessive egotism and detailed analysis of his own feelings sometimes become a little monotonous. He has however one poem which is so different from the others that it is refreshing as well as surprising. This poem represents the spirit of a dead wife returning and trying to comfort her husband, and especially urging him not to let his grief make the children sad;

> Grieve if you must, but not when they are there,
> When they come, let your cheeks be dry.

And in another verse she says,

> And when you kiss their tears away,
> Kiss them for their mother too.

In the works of Horace the delightful reminiscences of his own childhood are very familiar. There is that charming bit in one of the Odes telling how when a little child he once wandered off into the woods and " tired with play " he lay down under a tree and fell asleep. Then the doves came and covered him with leaves so that he was, as he says, " safe from serpents and bears." Everyone throughout the whole region heard about it and people wondered that no harm had befallen him, this *animosus infans*. In southern Italy where Horace was born the sight of a little child fast asleep under a tree is very common and may often recall this story. The fact that Horace never mentions his mother indicates that he had never known her, for there are many allusions to his father, his loving care and wise training. This father although he was a poor man had managed to save a little money, and not satisfied with the school at Venusia the town where they were living, he took his little boy to Rome, that he might have the advantages of the best city schools. Horace's description of the school at Venusia shows exactly how he remembered it, that school " where the great boys, sons of great centurions, used to go." We can imagine how very big those boys seemed to little Horace, for there is nothing bigger than a big boy in the eyes of a very small boy. In Rome the father used to escort his little son to school himself, just as we may often see an Italian father doing today. The desire of Horace's father was to give his son a liberal education, without any thought as to whether it might bring him material advantages or not, and he cared not who criticized him for this. He would have agreed with his son in some remarks which the poet made in later years about the " practical " theories of the Roman education of the day. The effect of those theories, like some of the so-called practical theories which prevail in America at the present time, was to set too high a value on mere money-getting, and fix the thought more on making a living than on that which is of far more importance, the making of a life. We may wonder if the father of Horace ever realized the genius of his child, but that we can never know, for he had died before the future poet began to write.

Seneca in writing to his mother gives an affectionate description of a little nephew, an irresistible child who was always so happy and so merry that no one, however sad, could remain sad when little Marcus was present. This little Marcus was probably the one who afterwards became known as the poet Lucan.

Juvenal, in bitter satire even, has a word of sympathy for the country baby who is taken to the theatre and is frightened by the actor's wide-mouthed mask. If Juvenal were in Rome today, he might sometimes be sorry for the babies who are taken to the theatre and also to concerts in the Colosseum. In another passage Juvenal refers to " the baby with his playmate the puppy," and there are many other references in Latin authors which indicate how common it was for Roman children to have pet animals.

Martial was especially fond of children and there are three well-known poems about a little slave girl whom he dearly loved. She was " sweet as the roses of Paestum," this little girl who would have been six years old if she had lived six days longer. This child was buried on Martial's farm at Nomentum, and the third poem about her was written years after she died, just before Martial returned to Spain, asking the next owner of the estate, whoever he might be, to take care of that little grave. There are various other poems referring to children among Martial's works.

From various sources we learn that it was customary for children even when quite young to be present in the dining room at the family meals, but they often had a separate table and a much simpler menu. At Pompeii we may still see a table in an out-of-door dining room which is believed to have been the children's table. There may also be seen in one of the houses more recently excavated at Pompeii some scratches on the wall of the dining room which are amusing now, but which must have caused annoyance rather than amusement when they were made, to the older members of the family at least. These scratches represent most extraordinary animals, and the place on the wall, the height from the floor, indicate approximately the age of the perpetrator who seems to have been trying to combine a horse and a pig into one beast. The remarks of *paterfamilias* when he discovered those things on the dining room wall may be left to the imagination.

Roman school-children frequently appear in Latin authors. Cicero in his letters often refers to his own children, and also to his nephew and to the little daughter of his friend Atticus to whom he sends many kisses. In one letter when young Marcus was about eleven years old, Cicero writes that he had decided to take the boy off to the country for the days of the games in Rome and have him spend that time in study. One cannot help feeling a little sympathy for Junior. That was one of the occasions when, to quote the Boston Herald, " a feller needed a friend." Cicero's daughter Tullia however generally had her own way with father, and he once changed all his plans for starting on a journey because Tullia wanted him to take her to the game. In one of the letters to his brother, Cicero has much to say about the boys' tutor whom he himself considered a most excellent teacher, " although," he adds, " the boys do say that he is frightfully cross." The somewhat extravagant language, *furenter irasci*, implies that Cicero is quoting the boys' own words.

When the poet Ovid was a boy and interested in literature, his father tried to turn him away from that study, using the same words which boys and girls who want to study Latin literature to-day often hear from those who try to persuade them to take something " practical " instead, " Why study a useless subject ? " As an unanswerable argument against the study of the classics, this Roman father often used to say to his son, " Even Homer left no property." Ovid's father was evidently a pedagogic modernist in his ideas, and in his opinion Homer was a failure.

Among the extant letters of Marcus Aurelius there are several written when he was a boy, some of which are very charming and show what a merry, as well as affectionate, boy he was. An early biography of Marcus Aurelius states that he was " solemn from his earliest childhood," but his own letters show that in his early years Marcus Aurelius was a genuine boy, and was not burdened by an excessive *gravitas*.

In the works of Ausonius there is a letter to his " Honey Grandson" who is just beginning to go to school, and grandfather gives Honey some very good advice about his studies. Ausonius once remarked that any praise bestowed on children is generally accepted by their parents as being gospel truth.

It is difficult to determine exactly the limit beyond which the word "children" should not be used, for the use of the word often depends more on the point of view of the speaker than on the exact age of those spoken of, and it is impossible to say just when the boy ceases to be a boy and becomes a man. A letter from Cicero's son when he was a student in Athens is decidedly boyish in some places. It is interesting to notice in this letter how young Cicero manages to indicate that he would like a larger allowance without making any direct request for it. He does not ask father for a check, not he, but he makes it very clear that a check would be most acceptable. The letter seems very modern too when we learn from it that there was one of his professors of whom Cicero Junior says that he was " really human."

Passages from Latin authors such as those which have been cited might be multiplied indefinitely, and readers of this paper will think of many which have not been included. But it is not from literature only that we may become acquainted with Roman children, for Latin inscriptions also furnish a rich source. Those children of whom we learn from tomb inscriptions do not seem to belong to the long ago, for the love and grief expressed are so intense that it brings them very near. In reading one after another of the many inscriptions which tell of little ones taken from the homes where they were so dearly loved, leaving the mother *maerentem, plorantem, et gementem,* we can hardly help feeling sympathy as if these people were personal friends. Children of all ages are to found here, including some whose lives had been extemely short. Of one it is said that she was a sweet little girl, *puellula dulcis,* who lived " half a year and eight days more, who bloomed and perished like a rose." Of one who lived only four hours it is said that he " lived just long enough to die." Another " just beheld the light, but it was so quickly snatched away from him that he did not live long enough to know why he had been born." Another very young baby was "snatched away from the very threshold of life. He was a little pet and although his life had been very short, he had inspired love that would be long." Of how many babies that might be said! There was a little boy of whom it is said that of the most affectionate children he was the most affectionate of all. For one little girl her father will grieve throughout the ages, *per saecula,* and of another we learn that her face and her speech were equally charming. Diminutives of endearment are frequently used. A little grand-daughter, for instance, is *nepotula cara,* or *nepotilla carissima.* It is interesting to notice how often the word *mamma* is used. While this is generally the baby word for mother, it sometimes refers to the grandmother or the nurse. One of the most pathetic epitaphs is on the tomb of a young mother of whom it is said that she carried with her into the other world the child who had just been born.

The inscription on the tomb of a boy of nine years recalls the childhood of Horace, since it is said of this boy that the father brought him up without the mother. Of pathetic interest too is the epitaph of a boy who died when away at school and the mother had his body taken home for burial. On this tomb, as on so many others, there are portraits of both mother and son. Another that arouses sympathy is the appeal of a soldier who has to leave his daughter buried in Spain. He begs his comrades to keep the light burning on that little grave, with the prayer that no one of them may ever suffer such grief. One inscription indicates that *Amor* was the pet name by which the child was called and no other name is given. Another little epitaph says to the reader, "If you want to know my name, think of the first month." In the vicinity of Naples the name *Ianuarius* was not uncommon. The inscription on the tomb of one small boy states that he was a good son who always obeyed his parents and died at the age of eight years. It is to be hoped that the apparent connection between the two statements was not intended.

A few deaths by accident are recorded. In one case a boy nine years old was killed in saving a younger brother from being run over by a carriage, and a very small child was run over by an ox-cart. Another child was accidentally killed by a little companion when they were playing.

The tomb inscription in the case of children as well as older people is sometimes put in the first person and includes remarks addressed to the passer-by. One says, " The whole house is in mourning, and if you had seen me, stranger, you too would shed tears at my death." Another, a baby of five months, asks, " Who could help feeling sad when he sees this sadness ? " But a little philosopher who had attained the age of seven years remarks that the fatal hour comes also to kings. Even the tombstone could not escape the punster. There was, for instance, a little girl whose name was Agatha Mater, and the inscription says, " Mater is my name, but *mater* I can never be." Agatha then goes on to tell us that her age was five years, seven months and twenty-two days, and then she adds, " While I lived, I played, and everybody loved me. I looked just like a boy, believe me, not a girl. I had red hair which I wore bobbed in front, long and loose in the back. I have a mother, but my father has gone before; so my death brings no suffering to him."

One of the most interesting inscriptions tells of a young person who " made fun of his grandmother." More than that he jeered at his uncle and he wheedled his grandfather, talking to him *pusilla voce.* The inscription goes on to tell what the neighbors said of him. Altogether he seems to have had rather a bad reputation, but when we read that this reprobate died at the somewhat immature age of two years, we may hope that if he had lived longer, he might have reformed. He must have been an extraordinarily precocious young person, for the inscription seriously affirms that although he had lived only two years, he knew as much as if he had lived sixteen.

Pride in the children who did well in school is very often expressed, and for indicating parental satisfaction the superlative *doctissimus* is none too strong and is frequently used. A very young girl, her mother's darling, is said to have excelled in all the liberal arts. She must have been a wonder. Of one small boy it is stated that he knew more than his teacher. There have been others of that kind and in more recent times a boy who was studying Greek learned Latin without being taught, and a little girl eight years old, if she had only lived long enough, would have been the most learned girl in the world. There are several others of whom a similar statement is made. It was only the early death, apparently, which prevented their having a world-wide reputation for learning. One inscription tells of a boy of thirteen who was awarded the prize at a competition of poets in Rome, and his native town, in grateful recognition of the distinction, honored him with a statue. We learn also of little Petronius Antigenides who, although he was only twelve years old when he died, had already studied the doctrines of Pythagoras, the poems of Homer, and all that Euclid taught, and had also " read books " evidently on other subjects. The reader might say that it was no wonder that he died young, were it not that the next line of the epitaph tells us that he liked play just as well as study. So, notwithstanding his early introduction to philosophy, we may hope that Petronius was an " all-round " boy. The frequent use of the adjective *rarissimus* indicates that the unusual children, those " uncommon children " of whom we often hear, were about as common then as they are now.

The inscriptions which have survived from the tombs of little slaves are noticeable, for the number of these is very large. One such child is said to have been a sweet little soul, *animula dulcissima,* and similar terms of endearment are frequently found. It was in some cases the parents of the child who erected the little tomb, but this was done more frequently by the master or mistress. Some of these inscriptions with their lavish expressions of affection recall the poems of Martial to which reference has already been made. There is one inscription on the tomb of a baby girl eight months old which furnishes a good illustration of the Roman love of title. It was the parents who erected the tomb in this case and the inscription states that the baby was the daughter of a slave of the Emperor Domitian. Then after Domitian's name two or three lines of his titles were added and thus quite an elaborate and impressive inscription was achieved. This is of special interest because there was a decree after Domitian's death that his name should be erased from all inscriptions. But when that decree was carried out no one thought probably of examining the tombstones of baby slaves.

Most of the inscriptions referring to children are those on tombs, but there are others also. One of the most significant is that on the Temple of Isis at Pompeii which states that this building was given to the city by a child six years old, and that in recognition of his munificence he was admitted to the rank of city councillor. It is of interest to notice that the parents of this six-year-old boy, by making their gift to the city in his name, paved the way for him to hold city offices later on, offices to which his father was not eligible because he was a freedman. This desire of parents to give their children a better start in life than they had had themselves was quite as common in the Roman Empire as it is in the United States. We may wonder whether this child and his parents were among those who perished in the destruction of the city, but we can never know.

One of the best ways of becoming acquainted with Roman children is by looking at them, and this we are able to do through the existing portraits. The making of portraits of children continued throughout the entire period of the Empire, and the number still in existence is very large. There are literally hundreds of bewitching little faces scattered through the museums of Europe which bear witness to the Roman fondness for children. Indeed in the whole realm of Roman portraiture there is nothing more attractive than these little Romans, many of whom are rendered with wonderful skill and understanding. Yet anyone who is interested in such portraits needs actually to search for them in the museum, for in many cases they are so inconspicuously placed, in dark corners or on high shelves, that they do not attract the attention of the casual visitor. Very few of these portraits have ever been photographed, and some of those of which there are photographs are far less attractive than many of the others. The attempts at identification which have been made are for the most part mere conjecture and little confidence can be put in any names which have been attached. In most cases there is no basis for identification, and it is probable indeed that the great majority are portraits of children whose names never became known to history. At one time there was a tendency to give names of Imperial families to some of these portraits without any real reason for such identification. There are, for instance, two little heads in the Vatican which were once arbitrarily called the grandsons of Augustus, and these names still cling to them although it was shown long ago that the heads could not have been made until nearly a century after the grandsons of Augustus were children. Yet the photographs bearing these names are still used as illustrations even in very recent textbooks. There are, however, a few cases in which an identification is possible, or perhaps even probable. One of these is a charming portrait of a little child now in Florence which has been called the " Baby Nero," and which bears sufficient resemblance to an authentic portrait of Nero when a man to give some ground for the conjecture, although it is by no means certain. Then there is that beautiful bronze boy in the Metropolitan Museum in New York, undoubtedly, so it is believed from the family resemblance, one of the princes of the Julio-Claudian family, and possibly one of the grandsons of Augustus. There are in existence a very few coin portraits of children which are especially interesting because they are so rare. A coin of Annius Verus at the age of seven has been used as a criterion in identifying two or three busts. There is also a coin portrait of Commodus when he was about six years old, or perhaps even younger since the Italian child often looks older than an American child at the same age. This is a charming portrait with a very bright, alert expression on the little face. A boy in Arles in Southern France has been called the young Marcellus as a child, but there seems to be no justification for that name. In one of the private collections in England there is a portrait of a little boy, a very attractive little fellow with round cheeks and curly hair, which has been identified with some degree of probability as Caracalla. One of the most beautiful of children's portraits, and one to which no photograph has done justice, is a little head now in the Barracco Museum in Rome. In looking at this sweet little face and learning that it was found at Prima Porta where the famous statue of Augustus now in the Vatican was found, one is reminded of that portrait of a child of Germanicus which Augustus used to keep in his bedroom and always kissed when he went into the room. The hair in this recalls Agatha's description of her red hair, being short in front and longer in the back of the neck, and in Copenhagen there is a boy's head which gives a still better illustration of that arrangement, the hair being quite long in the back. It will be remembered that Agatha says that she looked just like a boy. Children of all ages are to be found among the portraits, including several that are extremely young. The youngest probably is a baby now in Munich. This infant has a large head but not much hair, and his little face is so devoid of expression as to indicate that he had not been living long in this world when his portrait was made.   .

Besides the vast number of heads and busts there are also many interesting portrait statues of children. In the Torlonia collection for instance there is one of a little girl holding a pigeon close to her left side while she feeds it with her right hand. This little figure recalls the children feeding pigeons on Boston Common. Many portrait statues of Roman boys might be mentioned, several of them having a scroll in the hand and a book-box at the feet, indicating that they are schoolboys. Some of these fine boys make one think of Quintilian and his interest in such boys, for they doubtless look much as his youngest pupils used to look.

No less interesting than the portraits in the round are the innumerable portraits in relief on tombstones. In one of these now in the Palazzo dei Conservatori in Rome we see a boy who died of exhaustion because " neither morning nor evening could he be torn away from the Muses." The portrait with its haggard, weary little face looks just as we might expect. Young Quintus, although only eleven years old, had already gained distinction by a Greek poem read at a competition of poets held in the Capitol, and the proud parents had these verses inscribed on the tombstone. They wished to prove, as the inscription expressly states, that they had not exaggerated their son's achievement. But it can hardly be called very inspiring poetry, and most people after reading a few verses would be willing to take the parents' word for it rather than to read it all. It is interesting that the memory of this little Quintus Sulpicius Maximus has been perpetuated by the placing of a copy of the monument quite recently on the site where it was found near the Porta Salaria, and to-day the trams are constantly passing it. When one is in Rome, this copy is worth going to see.

The children on tombstones and sarcophagi, both portraits and other representations, are of special interest because they are often doing something, and thus illustrate facts learned from other sources also. A child " with his playmate the puppy," as Juvenal says, may be seen on many a tomb. Pet animals held an important place in the life of a Roman child and they are very often represented on tombs. Dogs and birds are especially common, but others also appear. One relief portrays a little girl feeding a bird which is perched on her left shoulder. Another shows a boy holding a bird on his left arm while he feeds it with his right hand. In another a dear little girl who wears a long tunic and a cloak is holding a kitten with both hands, and a cock standing by her is pecking at the kitten's tail. One little girl has a basket of fruit in one hand and a flower in the other. On another tomb we see a little girl holding fruit in one hand with her other hand resting on a great basket of grapes which stands beside her. There is a badly defaced relief in Verona which represents two children in a donkey cart with a little dog trotting along near the donkey. Portraits of children with their parents, one or both, are very common on tombstones. One example of this now in the Vatican collection has a child standing between his parents, with one hand on his father's arm and the other reaching out to the mother who is offering him fruit from a basket. An interesting one represents a man with a little child in his arms. The baby has an apple in his right hand and his left arm is around the father's neck. The attitude is very natural, and both the love of the father and the confidence of the child are very vividly portrayed. A tombstone now in the museum of Bonn has the figure of a man in military costume, with a smaller figure on each side. The smaller of the two, of which the inscription is lost, may perhaps have been the soldier's little son, and the other is shown by the inscription to have been a young slave. This relief recalls the many instances in which a slave was so completely a member of the family as to have a place in the family tomb. Tomb reliefs in which children are represented have been found in all parts of the Roman world. Unfortunately many of them are so broken or badly defaced that much interesting detail is lost. The sculpture in many cases is extremely rude, but lack of value from the point of view of art does not lessen the human appeal.

The figures of children in relief are not confined to tombs. It will be remembered how the procession of the Ara Pacis is enlivened by the presence of children and some of them are worth noticing in detail. There is the boy who is turning around to speak to the girl behind him and keeping his place in the procession by clinging to the toga of the man in front. Another boy, also turning to look back, is taking hold of the toga of the man before him apparently with both hands, while the hand of a woman in the background rests caressingly on his head. Then there is the little chap who is having difficulty in managing his toga which is too long for him, and his consciousness of it indicates that he is wearing it to-day for the first time. He had probably just been promoted to a toga in honor of the occasion. A younger kiddie still who is not burdened with any superfluous clothing is delightful. He is reaching up and trying very hard to attract the attention of two grown-ups. One of them holds him by the hand and he is pulling at the toga of the other, but they are both so absorbed in what they are looking at that they pay no attention to him. In some of the scenes on the Arch of Trajan at Benevento there are fine children. Two little boys are especially to be noticed each of whom is riding on his father's shoulders, and the way in which the little hand rests so lovingly on the father's head is very charming. The fathers are perhaps carrying them in this way so that the children may see the Emperor. In this scene there are other children also, one a baby in its mother's arms.

Many scenes of children playing may be found. On a child's sarcophagus, now in the Vatican, there are three groups of children playing with nuts, which give much interesting detail. There are many references in Latin literature to the use of nuts as playthings, and we learn from inscriptions that bequests to a town sometimes included a sum of money to provide nuts for all the children of the town, including the little slaves. On another sarcophagus we may see seven children in two groups, each group having a very lively game with balls. A sarcophagus now in the Louvre gives three scenes in the life of a child from the little baby to the schoolboy, and the rendering in all three is remarkably vivid. Another in the museum at Treves, shows two children working with their tutor, and a third, evidently coming late, is raising his hand asking permission to enter. This child's book-bag is worth noticing, for it looks so like those which we see to-day, and his little straight garment with long sleeves is very similar to the long-sleeved black aprons which are worn by little boys in France. The scene of one relief which has become hopelessly defaced was fortunately preserved by a drawing made long ago. This represented a very lively schoolroom with two teachers and numerous pupils.

There are many statuettes of children, some of which are of quite as much value as portraits perhaps in showing the feeling for the little ones. One of the best known of these is in the Capitoline Museum, a very small boy trying to put on a Silenus mask. The chubby little nude figure is very realistically rendered, and the child's difficulty in handling the mask, as well as the delight he is taking in it, are admirably portrayed. There is a charming one also in the Vatican, a little barefoot boy with his garment drawn up to hold some great bunches of grapes, and looking up with a very sweet and somewhat mischievous smile. Another little piece in the Vatican which is worth noticing is a bird's nest containing babies instead of birds. This nest of babies recalls a verse of Juvenal in which he speaks of how a father of three children " delights in his chattering nest."

There are many examples also of small bronzes of children, some of which are really exquisite. In the Museum of Archaeology in Madrid, there are a large number of terra cotta heads of children, including many of the Roman period, and some very charming ones among them. And a delightful little terra cotta piece may be seen in one of the collections in Germany, two school-children sitting close together, each holding a *diptychon* on his lap and busily writing an exercise.

Children asleep are to be seen in Roman sculpture, and there are many examples. Of these there is none more appealing than that dear little slave in the Museo delle Terme in Rome. In the Vatican there is a little fisherboy who has sat down and gone to sleep with his basket of fish on his arm. There are many examples of infants in swaddling bands, especially in tomb reliefs. Of these we may sometimes see replicas carried in the trams to-day, since the custom of using the bands still exists to some extent. An interesting piece now in the museum of Beaune in France is a child's cradle in terra cotta with the baby sound asleep and securely strapped in, and a dog curled up on the foot of the cradle is also asleep. In the British Museum there are several terra cotta models of cradles with infants in them.

In painting as well as sculpture there are many representations of children. Among the paintings from Pompeii now in the Naples Museum there is a series of small pictures with Cupids as children at play which are wonderfully vivid. In one scene where the game is hide and seek one little figure stands in a corner with his hands before his eyes, while the others are running off to hide. In another they are playing horse, one standing in a little two-wheeled chariot, and the other two being the horses. There are several other groups, in one of which they are playing in the hilarious manner of small boys, simply tumbling over each other and shouting, and when you look at the picture, you can almost hear the shouts. Two paintings of children which are now in the Vatican library should also be noticed. One of these apparently represents children preparing for a religious procession, and in the other the procession is about to start. In these groups each individual child is worth studying, and it is of interest also to notice various details in the dress. While the form of garments can be learned from sculpture, the paintings are of special interest because of the colors.

The sources for the study of Roman children are as inexhaustible in sculpture as in inscriptions, and in both subjects if one once begins the study, there is no place to stop.

The games which Roman children played at different ages might form the subject of a long chapter, so much can be learned in regard to them. Yet they did not differ so very much from those that children play to-day. Then, as always, imitating the grown-ups formed an important part of children's play. Plutarch in the Cato Minor refers to a birthday party where the children were playing law court, and it is related of Septimius Severus that when he was a boy the only game which he would play with other children was the game of judge, and he always insisted on being the judge himself. There have been other boys like that, but they have not all become Emperors.

The toys of the little Romans were much like those of modern times, and the first toys were presented at a very early period in the child's life. This was the *dies lustricus,* the day when the baby received its name. There was a fixed date for this, eight days after birth for a girl, and nine days for a boy, but the reason for the distinction is not known. Plutarch when he was in Rome could not find anyone who knew the origin of the custom, and so he includes it in his " Roman Questions." Plutarch himself suggests four quite different conjectures as possible explanations, but no one of them is satisfactory, and the real reason still remains unknown. The conferring of the name was a religious ceremony and was celebrated as a family festival. Relatives and friends assembled and brought gifts for the baby, gifts of every sort, but always including playthings. The first to be used was a rattle, *crepitaculum,* and of these there were various kinds. Toy animals of every description, balls and tops and kites, marbles, hoops, and little carts, all these the Roman children had and examples of them all are still in existence. Many dolls have been found and of many kinds, some being very simple while others show the most careful workmanship. In some cases the hair is so accurately rendered that it indicates the period when the doll was made. One for instance that was found at Ostia not many years ago is evidently a doll of the Antonine Age, as is shown by the hair. One toy which was very common was a wheel with a long handle attached. This was similar to the pair of wheels with a handle which Italian children use to-day, but unlike that in having no place where the child could put his foot. The single wheel with a handle also, just like the toy of Roman times, may still be seen in use in some parts of Italy. In old Tarquinia the author of this article was once called upon to serve as umpire in a race with these wheels exactly like those with which the little Romans of long ago used to play, and each small boy assured her that he could go faster than the others. The race was exciting, and the umpire followed the example of the shepherd umpire in one of Vergil's Eclogues and said,

> *Non nostrum inter vos tantas componere lites;*
> *Et tu dignus et hic.*

The little " savings-banks," as we call them now, boxes where small coins are put for safe-keeping, were evidently in use among the Romans, since more than fifty of them have been found, but no mention of them has as yet been found in any Latin author.

Of the toys of the Roman period a few examples may be found various museums, and in the British Museum there are many, : the Royal Ontario Museum of Archaeology in Toronto has a remarkable collection. These toys are most attractively arranged in a case by themselves which is known in the Museum as " The Children's Case," and here even the most casual visitor is sure to pause. That this case should arouse universal interest is natural, for " one touch of children's playthings makes the whole world kin." Among these Roman playthings there are balls and marbles, and also several tops which recall that passage in the Aeneid in which top-spinning is so vividly described. The toy animals ever dear to the childish heart are to be seen here in great variety, dogs of many kinds and some of them such intelligent dogs, horses and birds, a little bronze frog, two monkeys, one with a baby monkey on its back. There are dolls in abundance made of various materials including wood, bone, ivory, and terra cotta. One very fine terra cotta doll is nearly two feet tall and is said to be one of the largest dolls of the Roman period that has ever been found. In marked contrast to this aristocratic lady are two rag dolls. They are of most primitive construction and the stitches with which they are sewed are very conspicuous. But there is something especially appealing in these shabby old rag dolls whose dilapidated condition itself shows how hard they were played with by the little children who loved them nearly two thousand years ago.

Two objects in this case illustrate the eternal facility of the normal child in making playthings for himself, or enjoying something which has been very simply and hastily converted into a toy. One is a head of Apollo which was certainly never intended for a doll. But some child seems to have taken this old broken head and made it quite possible to dress it as a doll by fitting it with a stick and a rag. The other child-made toy is the neck of a broken glass bottle which was converted into a bell by the use of a small piece of wood, a little string, and a clapper of dried mud.

Quite as interesting as the toys perhaps are other things in the Toronto collection which belonged to children. There is a wooden writing-tablet with several lines written in imitation of a copy, evidently the work of a child just learning to write. He can make some letters fairly well, but gets queer effects in others. There are sandals so small that they must have been the first that the child ever wore, baby socks also, tiny bracelets and rings, little tunics and caps. In one of the little striped socks a minor detail may be noticed which is homely but human. This sock is mended in two places, one being where green and yellow stripes come together, the other where the colors are green and brown, and both places are mended with red yarn. Mother was in a hurry that morning and the red yarn was what she found first. There are tiny mittens also, and it may be noticed that the form of the little linen tunics is very similar to that seen in some of the marble reliefs.

The study of Roman children, like most other topics connected with life in the Roman period, grows more and more interesting the farther it is pursued. The more we learn of these children of an earlier day, the more vivid and alive do they appear, so that it does not seem that we are coming into contact with a by-gone age and making the acquaintance of little citizens of long ago, but rather that there is no long ago.

PLUTARCH IN HIS ESSAYS

There are few names of either Greek or Latin authors which are more familiar than that of Plutarch. No one would call Plutarch a great writer, and yet he has been better known than many who are greater, for Plutarch's Lives is one of the works which have never been lost sight of. It is a popular work in the best sense, one that appeals both to the scholar and to the general reader. The scholar may indeed find much to criticize in these biographies, but he will find the work worthy of criticism, and it will always be, as it has been, a work that can be read with no thought of study but simply because it is interesting. Plutarch's other works however, a voluminous collection of essays, have never been so universally known as the Lives, and one reason for this is that until very recently they have not been so accessible. There have been neither so many nor so convenient editions in the original, nor so many translations. Translations however, together with the original, are now appearing in the Loeb Classical Library.[1] It gives some idea of the number of these essays to know that they will fill fourteen volumes in this series.

There has been considerable writing about Plutarch in various languages, but of monographs dealing with his work as a whole there is even now nothing better than one by Archbishop Trench which was published over fifty years ago.

Although there have not been so many translations of the *Essays* as of the *Lives*, it is of some interest to notice that they have been translated into many languages and that translations were made very early. The earliest one known, so it is said, was made in the sixth or seventh century, in the Syriac language. After the invention of printing, Latin translations were printed before the Greek original.

[1] The translation is by Professor Babbitt of Trinity College, Hartford, Conn. There are also two small volumes of selected essays published by the Clarendon Press, one by Tucker in 1913, the other by Prickard in 1918.

Someone has remarked that it is the irony of fate that no one ever wrote a biography of Plutarch, the man who is remembered chiefly on account of the many biographies of which he was the author. But that is not to be wondered at, for no one ever had the material for a biography of Plutarch. Of his life certain definite facts are known, but all that is known has been culled from his own works and can be told in a few paragraphs. He was born about the middle of the first century A.D. at Chaeronea in Boeotia. It will be remembered that the Boeotians had the reputation of being extremely dull, and that Chaeronea was the scene of that great battle with the Macedonians (338 B.C.) in which Greek independence was lost nearly four centuries before Plutarch was born. It was at Chaeronea also that, about two hundred and fifty years later, the Roman general Sulla defeated the forces of Mithridates. Plutarch was therefore a native of the country which has the unusual distinction of becoming noted because of the dullness of its inhabitants, and he was born in a town which is known to history only as the scene of two lost battles.

Of the family of Plutarch little can be learned except that they were prominent people in the town. Plutarch himself received a good education, studied in Athens as well as other places, and travelled extensively. The exact date of his death, like that of his birth, is unknown, but it was certainly not before, and probably not long after the year 120. Thus he lived through the entire reigns of Nero, Galba, Otho, and Vitellius, Vespasian, Titus, and Domitian, Nerva, Trajan, and at least three years of Hadrian's reign. His life fell therefore in a very interesting and important period of the world's history, and included over twenty years of that century which Gibbon characterized as " the period in the history of the world during which the human race was most happy and prosperous." Plutarch was evidently a prominent man in Chaeronea. When he was quite young, but after he had already held several offices at home, he was sent to Rome as one of a delegation of two on an important mission to the proconsul of his province. This was probably his first visit to Rome, but after that he came here several times and seems to have spent much time here between the years 75 and 90. He came especially as a lecturer, and had a large acquaintance including people of importance, and made many friends. His references to Rome indicate how much he liked to be here. Plutarch loved Rome, the beautiful Rome, as he called it. He was evidently interested in all that was going on here, familiar with all the questions of the day, and enjoyed to the full the congenial companionship and the richness of his life in Rome. His travels however were not limited to his journeys to Rome. It is well known that the time when he lived was an age of travel. The main routes were safe, the facilities for transport were abundant, and transport was quite as rapid in Plutarch's time as it ever was before the days of steam. Travel was both easy and common, and Plutarch's interest in antiquity, his enthusiasm for archaeology, as well as his interest in the people of his own time took him all over Greece, to many parts of Italy, and to other countries of the Roman Empire also. Although Plutarch knew Rome so well, he never really learned the Roman language. That is not at all surprising, for while every educated Roman knew Greek, it was not uncommon for educated Greeks not to know Latin. Plutarch's lectures were of course given in Greek, and all his Roman friends undoubtedly spoke Greek. He says himself, in the introduction to his life of Demosthenes, that when he was in Rome he was so busy with public duties and with his many pupils in philosophy that he had not time to study Latin.

It seems a little strange at first that of the Latin authors who were his contemporaries Plutarch never mentions one, nor do any of these authors ever mention him. He does however refer to several people who were friends of the younger Pliny and among them Fundanus. That name is familiar to Pliny's readers especially through the beautiful letter which he wrote in regard to the death of Fundanus' young daughter. The letter is made very vivid by the fact that this girl's tombstone may now be seen in the Museo delle Terme. It will be remembered that Lanciani describes the finding of the tomb on Monte Mario. The father, Fundanus, appears several times in Pliny's letters and all that we can learn of him there makes it seem very appropriate that by Plutarch he is made the principal speaker in a dialogue on the control of anger. The fact that Pliny does not refer to Plutarch in any of his letters indicates that he was not personally acquainted with him. He may have heard some of his lectures but to him Plutarch was only one of the many Greek lecturers whom he heard here in Rome. As to Tacitus, I am inclined to think that even though they may have met, Plutarch and Tacitus would not have been particularly drawn to each other.

Although Plutarch apparently had an income that would have enabled him to live wherever he chose, although he had travelled so extensively and knew so many cities, although he so thoroughly enjoyed his life in Rome, he never thought of making his home anywhere except in the little town where he was born. The latter part of his life was spent almost entirely in Chaeronea, since after the year 90 he seems to have gone away for short trips only. It was a very dull little town and it may have been partly a sense of duty that kept Plutarch there, for he said that the town was already so small that he could not bear to make it smaller by the loss of a single citizen. At this time many Greeks were leaving their native towns and their own provinces to seek lucrative employment elsewhere under Roman patrons, and Plutarch was constantly urging his belief that men ought to try to raise the tone of the community where they lived instead of turning away from it. Thus in remaining in Chaeronea he was practicing what he preached. He seems moreover to have really enjoyed life in the little town instead of having been depressed by it, and that indicates that he had resources in himself which would have made it possible for him to find interests anywhere. He does however lament the lack of a public library such as larger cities had. Some of the German critics have ridiculed Plutarch's local patriotism, but to me it is one of his most endearing characteristics. His readers moreover may be very glad that he did remain in Chaeronea, for he gives valuable pictures of life in a small town in the second century A.D. such as are not to be found elsewhere.[2]

Plutarch was as loyal to the Roman Empire as he was to his own town. Like many other provincials he wrote of the Roman Empire with unstinted praise. He did not simply accept it as inevitable, he was enthusiastically appreciative of the blessings which the Pax Romana brought to the provinces. It may be surprising to find that Plutarch has a good word even for Nero.

---

[2] Chaeronea was destroyed by an earthquake about 551 A.D. and was never rebuilt.

He was a student in Athens at the time when Nero made his celebrated visit to Greece and he seems to have retained a certain affection for Nero's memory derived from what he saw and heard of him at that time. One reason probably why Plutarch used the form of Parallel Lives in his biographies was that his love of Greece and his admiration for Rome were both so great that he could not bear to make either more prominent than the other in this work. Plutarch's life in Chaeronea was quiet but busy. He was a man of affairs, keenly interested in all that pertained to the welfare of the community, and always ready to give his time and energies to the interests of the community. But first of all Plutarch was a teacher, one who found joy in his teaching and who took his teaching seriously whatever the subject. A delightful teacher he must have been, and in some respects, perhaps, a great teacher. He lived at a time when there was leisure for the cultivation of the humanities, when students were not urged to drop the study of the classics and take something " practical " instead, when knowledge could be sought for its own sake without thought of any material advantage which the possession of knowledge might bring. He was an eminently sociable being living in a very sociable age, a man who enjoyed society, who considered intercourse with his kind one of the best things in life. His extensive travels, the fact that he had seen the cities of so many men and learned their customs, gave him an understanding of mankind and a capacity for sympathy hardly possible for anyone of less broad experience. The reader of Plutarch can hardly fail to be reminded of that frequently quoted verse in Terence, " I am a man, there is nothing human that does not concern me." *Homo sum ; humani nil a me alienum puto.* It is indeed the humanity of Plutarch, his large-heartedness, that more than anything else has endeared him to posterity and made him a name that from his own time down to the present has never been forgotten.

In the amount of his writings Plutarch may be compared with Varro and the Elder Pliny. Of the biographies fifty have come down to us and there were others which have been lost. Of the essays about eighty are extant, and there is reason to believe that these are not more than half of the original number. The traditional title which has been given to these essays, and it is impossible to know when or by whom it was first given, is *Moralia*, and this title is commonly translated, " Moral Essays," or simply " Morals." " Moral Essays " is not a very alluring title, and it certainly gives no reason to expect light sketches, in some cases amusing, such as one likes for a half-hour after dinner. It gives no idea of the miscellaneous character of the work and of the great number of subjects treated. No one would suppose from the title that we should find here talks on music, politics, talkativeness, education, curiosity, the laws and customs of the Lacedaemonians, and the preservation of health; discussions of good manners, and of the question whether dumb animals have reason; discourses on natural science, and accounts of dinner-parties. Nor would anyone suspect from the title the special value of these works, their chief value, I might say, for the pictures they give of the everyday life of ordinary people in the early Roman Empire. It is quite true that in all of Plutarch's works the moral note is very prominent, but the title *Moralia*, if used at all, might be used of the biographies just as well as of the Essays.

Among all these works of Plutarch it may be noticed that there are few of which the authorship has been even questioned, and very few in regard to which there is any agreement among critics that they are spurious.

In the writings of Plutarch there are many glimpses of his own home life and it is interesting to notice that his wife had more freedom than was common for Greek women even in that late period. She received guests, made visits, attended banquets with her husband almost as freely as a Roman woman apparently. Yet that Plutarch's ideas as to the higher education of women did not differ essentially from those of most Greeks, may be inferred from his comment on Cornelia, the brilliant wife of Pompey. This young woman, he says, was well educated in literature, music, mathematics, and philosophy, and then he adds that although she was so well educated, she was " free from that disagreeable officiousness which such learning generally gives to young women."

From such voluminous works as these essays of Plutarch it is difficult to know which ones to choose for brief notice. The *Symposiacs* or *Table-Talks* is one of the most interesting and also one of the longest, there being nine books of it. This is dedicated to Plutarch's Roman friend Sosius Senecio, one of the friends of Plutarch whom we meet also in Pliny's letters. In the introduction the author speaks of gathering up some of the scattered topics which he and Senecio had discussed and had heard discussed at various dinner-tables both in Rome and in Greece, and implies that it was at the suggestion, or perhaps the request, of Senecio that the work was written. It is probable therefore that many of these discussions are to a certain extent reports of actual conversations in which Plutarch had taken part. In several of them Senecio also appears as a speaker but not in all. The fact that the same people appear over and over again indicates that most of these parties took place at Chaeronea. A few however are located at Eleusis after the celebration of the Mysteries, at Delphi, and at Galepsus, a Greek watering-place. Among the guests we find some interesting people including a historian, a mathematician, a physician, and a Stoic philosopher. This man whose name was Themistocles is said to have been a descendant of the great Themistocles. There were also teachers of literature and an archaeologist. In short they were, many of them, people who were " doing things," as we sometimes say. In the *Table-Talks* the reader soon begins to feel acquainted with various members of Plutarch's own family. He had a large family connection and we meet some of his relatives again and again. His father and his grandfather, his brother and his sons, appear frequently. It is rather noticeable that these young men and their great grandfather go to the same parties. There are others also who appear from time to time and the reader soon begins to feel that he is in the company of educated and interesting people. The topics are many and of great variety. One of the first discussions is on the question of what kind of topics are suitable for dinner-table conversation, with the very obvious conclusion that it depends on the company, for the topics like the wine, he says, should be something of which everyone may partake. Another question discussed at some length is the placing of guests at a dinner-table. Since the success of the occasion depends so much on having people together who enjoy each other, the question is raised whether it is better that places be assigned by the host, or that guests be left free to choose their own. This discussion is mainly between Plutarch's brother who approves the latter plan, and his father who holds to the former. The brother declares that in a large company any arrangement of guests that will be entirely satisfactory to everybody is always difficult and often impossible, and that it is much easier for the host, and also more " democratic," as he says, to make no assignment of places. The father does not agree at all with his son, and says that a host who does not assign places is shirking his responsibility. He quotes the famous Roman general Aemilius Paulus who on one occasion, when he was giving much time and thought to the placing of guests at a banquet, remarked that it needed quite as much planning to place the guests at a dinner-table as to place the troops for a battle. When this discussion between his father and his brother became rather vigorous, Plutarch was asked to say with which of the two he agreed. This he avoided doing by making the safe reply that it depended on circumstances. As he goes on however it becomes evident that his opinion was the same as that of his father. In speaking of his own method he said that whenever he found difficulty in deciding to which one of two or more guests he should give what is called the place of honor, he always gave it to his own father if he was present, and if not, he gave it to his grandfather, or his uncle, or his father-in-law. It would seem as if someone must have remarked at that point that not everyone is so rich in elderly relatives as to be able to adopt such a plan as this. The discussion is prolonged with various people taking part, and in reading it one is constantly reminded of how easy it is to form theories, and how difficult it often is to follow those theories in practice. Plutarch's opinion was that it is best to abandon ceremony as to rank, but take great care to have people together who will find each other congenial. " For your next neighbor at table," he says, " you would always prefer a villain if he is interesting, rather than a bore, however worthy." The variety of topics in the *Table-Talks*, like the variety in the essays as a whole, is almost endless. There are discussions, for instance, on the questions whether it is suitable to wear wreaths and flowers at the table, whether wrestling is the oldest exercise, why old people hold a book at a distance, whether men or women are the more hot-tempered, why signet rings are regularly worn on the fourth finger, whether the Jews abstained from swine's flesh because they worshipped that animal, or because they had a natural aversion to it, and what kinds of music are most suitable for a dinner-party. Superstitions are among the subjects discussed, and when most of the company are ridiculing the superstition of the " evil eye," one man ventures to express his opinion that after all there may be something in it. He has had many successors. Thus the conversation runs on and on, taking up one question after another, and in some cases the discussions are so prolonged that the reader begins to wish for a change of subject. Among the topics discussed there are some that seem hardly suitable for a dinner-party, although Plutarch himself says " what we used to talk about might be freely told to everybody." He protests against the idea that serious subjects are entirely out of place at the dinner-table, and says that to banish philosophy from the conversation would be worse than putting out the lights in the dining-room. Plutarch refers in one passage to a saying which he frequently used to hear in Rome to the effect that while one may take his dinner alone if necessary, it is impossible to really dine except in company. He thinks also that the most enjoyable dinner-parties are those which are not too large, and quotes with approval the advice of his grandfather who used to say, " Entertain often with few guests at a time."

The *Dinner-Party of the Seven Sages* also contains much vivacious conversation, but it is very different from the *Symposiacs*. In the *Symposiacs,* as we have seen, there are glimpses of actual dinner-parties in the second century A.D., while the *Dinner-Party of the Seven Sages* is of course purely imaginary. There was an ancient tradition that the Seven Wise Men of Greece once met at Delphi, and that on another occasion they were all entertained by Periander at Corinth. With this tradition only as a basis Plutarch wrote the story. At the party there were present the Seven Sages and seven other people who had been invited to meet them, and the conversation is sometimes very lively. At one point Solon remarks that it would be a great convenience if the human being did not need food. But this idea is vigorously opposed by another guest who says that to dispense with food would be doing away with the Gods of Friendship and Hospitality, and entertainment and hospitality, he declares, are the most humanizing and essential elements in our mutual relations. The reader finds here some of the old stories with which he is familiar, for instance, the one of the young man who threw a stone at a dog but hit his stepmother, and remarked, "Not such a bad aim, after all." The party broke up with a quotation from Homer which Solon repeated to indicate that it was time to go, "Night-time advances apace; 'tis well to pay heed to the night-time." A German critic thinks that this essay is not by Plutarch, but that theory is not accepted by English scholars, because the style is so thoroughly Plutarchian.

Some of Plutarch's essays of a more formal character were delivered first as lectures. There are certain ones of which we may be sure that that was the case, and others which may or may not have been used as lectures. There is one on Friendship which it is interesting to compare with Cicero's essay on the same subject. Plutarch was so happy in his own friends that he was eminently fitted to write on Friendship, which is, as he said, "the most pleasant and delightful thing in the world." This essay is worth reading although much of it may seem rather trite. Closely connected with this are two others, *How to Tell a Flatterer from a Friend*, and *How to Profit by One's Enemies*. His characterization of a flatterer at his worst is not unlike that which Juvenal gives in one of his satires when he is saying that it is of no use for any Roman to try to vie with the Greeks in that profession. Plutarch takes up also the more subtle kinds of flattery which are not so easily detected. The essay on *How to Profit by One's Enemies* also has some good things in it. Plutarch accepts the fact that it is sometimes impossible to avoid making enemies, remarking that even friendships may sometimes involve a man in enmities. But he thinks that enmities may be very useful, and quotes the philosopher who said that to keep straight anyone needs either very good friends or red-hot enemies.

The article on *Political Precepts* is full of good advice to a statesman, precepts which apply quite as well to the present day as to the time when Plutarch wrote.

There is a short discussion of the *Three Kinds of Government*, monarchy, oligarchy, and democracy, showing Plutarch's own opinion that, all things considered, monarchy was probably the best. The essay on *Old Men in Public Life* is full of good things

and well worth reading entire. In this he remarks very truly
that reputation is like fire in that it is much more easily kept
alive than rekindled after it has become cold, and that life and
the life worth living should end together. One noted man is
quoted as saying that if he were not busy, there would not be
anything to distinguish him from his servants. Plutarch quotes
also that well-known remark of the elder Dionysius who, when
he was asked one day if he had any time to spare, replied, " Time
to spare? Heaven forbid that I ever should! "

There is an essay on the preservation of health, *Advice about
Keeping Well,* which contains much common-sense advice in
regard to rational living, and many of his precepts apply just
as well to one age as another. This begins as a dialogue, but the
dialogue form is very soon dropped. He remarks that some
people when they are not well fail to take the precautions they
should, because they are unwilling to admit that they are not
well. They will not rest when they are tired because they do
not want anyone to know that they are tired. He enlarges somewhat on the folly of this, and then has much to say on the folly
of the opposite extreme, which, as he says, will result in making
unnecessary care necessary. Giving excessive attention to the
body lessens the self-respect of the soul. One should handle
his body like the sail of a ship, not lower it when the weather is
fine, but be careful if there are indications of a storm. It is a
mistake to become so bound to one routine of life that you
cannot depart from it without trouble. Plutarch also emphasizes
the fact that health is not to be purchased by idleness and inactivity. The man who thinks he can conserve his health by doing
nothing, he says, is like one who would guard his eyes by not
seeing, and his voice by never speaking. Plutarch has much
to say in this essay about exercise and also in regard to diet, and
another entire essay is devoted to the use of meat as a food.
Some of the arguments which he advances against this are the
same as those used by vegetarians of modern times.

Another of the very practical essays is in the form of a letter
addressed to a Bride and Groom, *Praecepta Coniugalia.* This
was an actual letter sent as a wedding present, " with Plutarch's
best wishes," to two of his young friends who had just been
married. That Plutarch's ideas in regard to the position of the

wife were Greek, rather than Roman and modern, is of course
to be expected, and they may be illustrated by a few sentences.
" The property of the family," he says, " should be considered as
belonging to the man, even though the wife contributes the larger
share." " A wife should do her talking either to her husband,
or through him." The subordinate position of the wife is
emphasized throughout, but aside from that much of the advice
given on both sides is excellent.

Leaving now these extremely practical subjects, we will notice
some of those which deal with literature. There is extant an
abstract of a comparison of Aristophanes and Menander which
is very entertaining. It is a little surprising to find that Plutarch
considers Menander by far the greater of the two. The article
is of interest in confirming what we learn from other sources of
the universal popularity of Menander. Plutarch declares that
there was no one who had any knowledge of the Greek language
who did not enjoy Menander, and that the theaters never had
in the audience more men of culture and reputation than when
Menander's plays were given. Aristophanes on the other hand
is said to be " harsh and coarse." Plutarch criticizes his style,
says that his characters are overdrawn, and that he cannot understand why Aristophanes had such a great reputation. But
Menander's plays, he affirms, " partake of a divine salt, as if they
were made of the very sea out of which Venus sprang," and
Menander's poetry, he declares, is " the most universal ornament
that was ever produced by Greece." It is always refreshing to
find an author who is not afraid to give utterance to his enthusiasms, or to disagree with the majority. But reading this comparison one is reminded that Aristophanes has often been called
an " elusive poet," for he certainly seems to have eluded Plutarch.

Another rather amusing article is entitled, *The Malice of
Herodotus*. This was inspired probably by some of Herodotus'
remarks about the Boeotians. Plutarch felt called upon to defend
his ancestors, and he is very vigorous in his defence. He accuses
Herodotus of incorrect statements, of narrating facts in such a
way as to give false impressions, and of deliberately assigning
bad motives to actions the real motives of which neither he nor
anyone else could possibly know. He is a little sarcastic in
wondering if Herodotus was the only person of his time who

knew anything about Greek history. Various passages from Herodotus are cited in support of these criticisms.

Another essay which furnishes some entertaining reading is in the form of a dialogue between Odysseus and one of Circe's victims. Odysseus has implored Circe to restore to human shape the men whom she has changed into animals. Circe replies that she is quite willing to do so if they really want it, but says that Odysseus would better ask them first if they do desire it. Accordingly a pig who has retained the faculty of human speech is brought in and he and Odysseus proceed to discuss the question. Most of the talking is done by the pig who claims that in many respects animals are far superior to man, in courage for instance, in temperance, simplicity of living, and especially in contentment. In regard to courage he argues that it is sometimes said of a brave man that he is as bold as a lion, but who ever said of a lion that he was as bold as a man? He claims also that animals use reason quite as much as man. Odysseus does not find much to say in reply to the individual arguments, but his final remark is to the effect that he cannot admit that any beings have reason if they do not recognize Deity.

The essay on *Curiosity* is very lively. The gossip, Plutarch says, is content to remain ignorant of many things that are worth knowing, but eager to learn about the misdeeds of his neighbor's grandfather. The scandal-monger finds no pleasure in scandals which are stale, but wants them hot and fresh. There is in this essay a remark on custom-house inspectors which sounds very modern. Plutarch says that we are annoyed and indignant at the collector of customs, not when he imposes duty on articles which are openly imported, but when he gets our baggage all out of order in searching for hidden articles. "But even this," he adds, "the law authorizes the inspector to do."

Rather closely connected with this essay is the one on *Talkativeness*. In this Plutarch discusses among other things the subject of answering questions. Three different ways of answering a question are considered, the barely necessary, the polite, and the superfluous, and these he illustrates by answers to the question, "Is Socrates at home?" If the answer is simply, "No," that is all that is really necessary; the one who asked the question learns what he wanted to know. But the brusqueness of the reply leaves an unpleasant impression, and the polite answer would add a few words, for instance, " No, Socrates is not at home, but you might find him at the bankers." That is a more agreeable reply to receive than the other, even though it makes no difference to you where Socrates is, if he is not at home. But the way in which a talkative person, who likes to tell all he knows and is incapable of conciseness, might answer the question, Plutarch illustrates in this way, as an example of a superfluous reply. " Is Socrates at home? " " No, but you will find him at the bankers waiting for some strangers from Ionia, concerning whom he has had a letter from Alcibiades, who is now near Miletus staying with Tissaphernes the Satrap of the Great King, the same who used formerly to help the Lacedaemonians but who is now attaching himself to the Athenians, thanks to Alcibiades; for Alcibiades is anxious to be recalled from exile and is trying his best to persuade Tissaphernes to change sides." (One sentence.) In fact, Plutarch says, he will go on talking until he has poured the whole eighth book of Thucydides over the listener, and war has been declared with Miletus and Alcibiades has been exiled a second time. There are many good passages in this essay, but it must be admitted that in his discussion of garrulity Plutarch sometimes becomes a little garrulous himself.

Among the writings of Plutarch two personal letters are to be especially noticed. One is a letter of sympathy to his friend Apollonius who has lost a son. This is over-flowing with quotations some of which are extremely long. The use of quotation is indeed characteristic of Plutarch, but in this letter the number and length of the quotations are both excessive. The letter moreover does not have the finish of most of Plutarch's writings. These two facts combined have given rise to the theory that what has come down to us is not the finished letter, but a rough draft for it, and that the author had collected a great mass of quotations some of which might be used, leaving the selection to be made in the revision. This theory, if correct, gives an additional value to the letter, for it shows something of Plutarch's methods of composition. The extracts from earlier authors are really the most important part of the work, for many of them are not found elsewhere. The revised form of the letter would doubtless have been much better, and yet it is perhaps more valuable in its present condition. There are admirable passages here and there and much of what Plutarch says is just what is still found in similar letters. There is also extant a very tender and beautiful letter written to his wife when their little daughter died, Plutarch himself being away from home at the time. This letter is of special interest for the picture which it gives of Plutarch's wife, as well as showing his own tenderness.

The essay on *Tranquillity of Mind* is one of the finest. Plutarch himself had attained tranquillity of mind to such a degree that he can impart something of it to his readers. He makes it very clear that serenity is not to be gained by idleness and inactivity, that nothing conduces more to tranquillity of mind than occupation and interests.

The *Roman Questions* (*Quaestiones Romanae*) is one of the works of Plutarch which has aroused much interest. This has been called "the earliest formal treatise on the subject of folklore," for, although Plutarch was not the first to propound such questions, he was the first to publish a collection of them. In this work a hundred and thirteen questions on Roman customs are discussed, many of them concerning religious rites. The questions are not answered, and indeed if Plutarch had known the answer, the question would not have been included. He does however suggest what he considered possible explanations, and frequently several different explanations for each question. But many of his conjectures are very far-fetched, and in some cases he starts with assumptions rather than facts. He seems to assume, for instance, that many of these customs were instituted intentionally and deliberately by men who had themselves studied antiquities and had as much learning as he had. Some of Plutarch's suggestions are of interest however, not because they answer the question proposed, but because they arouse other questions in the mind of the reader. Mistakes are to be found in some of Plutarch's remarks on Roman customs, but that is not surprising, since mistakes are inevitable for anyone who writes of the customs of foreigners without a thorough knowledge of the language of the people about whom he is writing. That Plutarch's knowledge of Latin was very imperfect, he says himself, as we have already noticed, and it would be evident even without his own statement to that effect. He picked up enough of the language in his visits to Rome to enable him to speak it with some degree of fluency, though often incorrectly, and to understand it when it was spoken distinctly. He acquired sufficient facility in reading Latin to enable him to use Latin sources in his writing, although he did not always use them with exactness, and it is evident that he did not know Latin well enough to read it for pleasure. Mistakes in translation sometimes occur, and we occasionally find one of those literal translations which, although they are absolutely literal, are wholly incorrect because they fail to give the meaning of the original, showing that the translator simply did not see the point.

The questions proposed are of a miscellaneous character, including the following: —

Why was the number of torches used in a wedding ceremony invariably five?

Why were walls sacred, but gates not?

Why did they make the month of January the beginning of the New Year?

Why did they fasten straw to the horns of savage bulls?

Why did nobles wear crescents on their shoes?

Why did the Romans compute the beginning of the day from midnight?

Why was the month of May considered an ill-omened month for weddings?

Why is Janus represented as having two faces?

Why in the naming of children were the names of boys invariably given on the ninth day after birth, while it was the eighth day after birth for girls?

It is probable that the *Roman Questions* was a work of Plutarch's old age, and it is certain that it was not written in Rome.

The two subjects on which Plutarch's opinions are of the most interest at the present time are education and religion. Education in the early centuries of the Roman Empire was the subject of much thought and much discussion, quite as absorbing to many people as it is to-day. In this period education was at an interesting stage, especially so because of the intermingling of Greek and Roman ideas, and the conflicting claims of rhetoric and philosophy. The rivalry of these two continued for a long time, and it may be remembered that the tutor of Marcus Aurelius was much distressed because his pupil became more interested in philosophy than he was in rhetoric. There was constant discussion of theories and methods among educators, and there were then, just as there are now, many theories all of which sounded well, many of which seemed to be excellent in themselves, but which did not harmonize with each other. It may be said in general that the prevailing aim in education was culture, mental, moral, and social. Subjects of a purely utilitarian nature, " practical subjects " as they are sometimes called to-day, were not considered as having any place in the liberal curriculum. The number and variety of subjects on which Plutarch wrote shows how wide was the range of his own interests, and this breadth of interest was a characteristic of the Greco-Roman education in the time of the Empire. Plutarch, who was an active teacher and not merely a writer on education, possessed to an eminent degree one essential for successful teaching, an intense interest in his fellow-men as individuals. He emphasizes the pupil's own responsibility, the fact that whatever the teaching may be, whether good, poor, or indifferent, whatever the teaching is, it is the student himself who must do the learning. He was enough of a teacher too to know that there is nothing more uninspiring, nothing much worse on the part of a teacher than a pedagogic attitude. Plutarch undoubtedly emphasized the moral instruction in his teaching and it may be that he sometimes carried it too far. The result of that is likely to be, of course, one of two things. The pupil either becomes too much absorbed in moral questions, excessively introspective and self-centered, or else he revolts against the whole subject and does not want to hear or think of moral questions. If Plutarch did carry it too far, there were probably among his hearers both those who went to one of these extremes and those who went to the other.

One thing on which Plutarch constantly insists is the cultivation of good manners. He has so much to say on the subject of politeness that it would be possible to compile a handbook on etiquette composed entirely of Plutarch's precepts. Some of his advice is indeed so extremely elementary as to seem unnecessary, but the emphasis put on politeness shows that those old Greeks were as courteous as they were wise, and that they recognized the importance of good breeding rather more fully perhaps than is always the case in modern times.

The importance of the right reading, especially for the very young, is stressed, and there is a full discussion of how to study poetry. In regard to the study of mathematics Plutarch makes one rather surprising statement. He is urging that girls should study mathematics, because, he says, it is a study that " tends to keep a woman from foolish practices." Then he adds that no girl would want to dance when she was learning geometry. Most of us have never observed that the study of geometry has any such effect on girls, and we should be very sorry if it had. In fairness to Plutarch it really ought to be said that this was not his only reason for advising the study of mathematics.

There is an essay entitled *The Student at Lectures,* as one translator words it, which is of special interest. This is in the form of a letter addressed to one of his young friends and contains many good things. The mind, he says, is not a receptacle that calls for filling, but it is like the wood ready for a fire, which needs only kindling to start the flame. " Some young people are so ill-informed as to suppose that lack of restraint is the same thing as freedom." " With right-minded people coming of age does not mean rejection of rule, but change of ruler." " How many false and even pernicious doctrines we accept because we esteem and trust their exponent! " Plutarch urges that it is a great mistake to cultivate the art of speaking before learning how to listen. On this point he puts much emphasis, affirming that anyone who cannot listen may do much talking, but seldom has anything to say that is worth hearing. He refers to various kinds of lectures and discusses the difference between the highly specialized and the popular. He said of lectures what the Elder Pliny said of books, that there are none so bad that they do not contain something good. (A statement that is perhaps open to question in both cases.) In this article Plutarch is speaking from the point of view of the lecturer and he emphasizes his need of the attention of the audience. A negligent attitude on the part of the student he considered a social crime. The class-room, he says, is very much like a ball game. It is useless for the thrower to do his part unless the catcher does his. Good hearers, he declares, are just as necessary for a successful lecture as congenial guests are for a successful dinner-party. Some of Plutarch's remarks in this essay would cause any college professor to chuckle. When he sets forth the different types of students for instance, we see that he knew them all. He had had experience with both the diffident who have not the courage to ask the questions that they need to ask, and with the over-confident who take much more than their share of the class-room time. He was acquainted with the indifferent, the would-be *blasé,* those who lean back in their seats and by their attitude virtually say to the professor, " Now interest me if you can." He knew also the excessively enthusiastic, that is, those who are bubbling over with enthusiasm, but have no discrimination and no very clear idea of what they are enthusiastic about. He referred to those who tried to show off by propounding difficult questions to the lecturer, and those who delayed progress in the class-room by asking foolish or superfluous questions. Students who repeatedly put to the teacher questions which would be quite unnecessary if they had done any real work themselves, are compared to unfledged birds which expect to receive everything ready prepared. Plutarch had had experience too with the most satisfactory of all students, those who have ability, interest, and ambition, and he realized that the good teacher is like the good doctor in that he often shows his skill by making himself unnecessary. Plutarch's view of the business of the student may be summed up very briefly : it consists in getting an intelligent grasp on valuable instruction and in cultivating the power of independent thinking together with the acquisition of knowledge.

In regard to religion, all that Plutarch has to say is of interest in revealing the man himself, and his views are also of great importance in a study of the religious beliefs and the religious life of the early Empire. This is a fascinating subject of study because of the revival of moral earnestness and religious feeling which was concurrent with the establishment of the Empire, and was in striking contrast to the flippancy and the recklessness which had characterized the last years of the Republic. Paganism in Plutarch's time was still the accepted faith of millions of people, and it aroused at that time a passionateness of devotion which was hardly known perhaps before Christianity challenged it. We should remember that Paganism in the early centuries of the Empire was the " faith of the fathers," that its antiquity contributed to its vitality, and to the feeling, the belief, that it must and ought to be handed on to posterity. Plutarch's beliefs must be culled from many of his works and could not be set forth in a few paragraphs. His conception of religion has been described in this way, " *a philosophical monotheism with loopholes for polytheism,*" characterized by " *calm rationalism and gentle piety.*" This would answer as well as any other definition, perhaps, if we must try to define it in a single sentence, but defining it in a single sentence is impossible. There are certain points in his belief however that may be stated briefly. It is evident that Plutarch believed in a personal Deity, in the power of God, in the goodness of God, in the care of God for mankind, and in his help in all human life. He depicts God as a father, and he has the feeling of there being an intimate relationship between Divinity and the human heart. No service, he says, is more acceptable to the heavenly powers than to think rightly of them, to believe that they are friends to man, saviours not destroyers. He taught that a knowledge of truth is the greatest blessing that can be given to man. He believed that Nature is the work of God, that it is not Nature that should be worshipped, but God in and through Nature. A good man, he says, should consider every day a festival, " for the world is the most august of temples and the most worthy of its Lord." It is possible that in some respects Plutarch may have been a little in advance of the trend of his time, yet it becomes evident to the reader that for the most part he is depicting the aims and aspirations of the people around him. He does not speak as one standing alone, but as one of many who hold the same beliefs.

Among Plutarch's works there is a long discussion of the worship of Isis and Osiris which is of value for anyone who wishes to study those oriental religions which for so many centuries found favor in Rome and throughout the Empire. There is an essay on *Superstition* which has been well called a sermon. The one on *Virtue and Vice* too has been called an excellent sermon, and there are several others to which that name might be given. Under *Superstition* both superstition and atheism are discussed. Plutarch himself has no sympathy with either the one or the other, but he considers that of the two superstition, which is, as he says, " the most incapacitating of all fears," is the more pernicious. It is worse, he believes, to hold utterly false conceptions of Deity, than to believe that there is no Deity. This conviction of Plutarch, that even atheism is less deplorable than superstition, was very shocking to the Church writers of the Renaissance and brought much criticism upon him. The breadth of Plutarch's religious teaching may be inferred from the fact that some of the early Church writers borrowed from him very freely, although they did not in all cases acknowledge the debt.

Among the essays of Plutarch, while there are some of real importance, there are many that will seem to the reader very unimportant. But it is in just that fact that the value of some of these essays consists. There is so much of the commonplace in human life that there is nothing more useful than the commonplace for becoming acquainted with the people of an earlier age.

As to style, Plutarch has been underrated, and the same thing is true of many other authors of the Roman Empire both Greek and Latin. That old idea that there is nothing in Greek literature worth reading since the beginning of the present era, and that there is no Latin author worth reading later than Tacitus, is one of the worst of fallacies. Plutarch himself has a comment on that theory. He says that refusing to read any authors except those who wrote in pure Attic style is like refusing to wear a thick coat in cold weather unless the wool came from pure Attic sheep. Those classical scholars who are not acquainted with the literature of the Roman Empire lose much that is of great interest. Although the later authors do not have the perfection of style which characterizes the writings of the Golden Age, any lack of that kind in their works is more than atoned for by the human interest. As to Plutarch's style, we may notice that it is often dramatic, although he never wrote drama, that he sometimes uses very successfully a poetic manner of presentation, although he did not write poetry, and that, whatever criticisms may be made on his style, he is always readable, for he could take any subject and present it in an interesting way. His style is often conversational in character, and reading some of the essays one is constantly reminded of what a delightful man he must have been to talk with. His writings all bear the impress of the man. Through the essays we may see Plutarch in his own family, in his town, in his country, and as a citizen of the Roman Empire, and we see that his sympathy and his understanding were not confined to family, or town, or country, or Empire, but were universal. After a little time devoted to the essays, the reader will begin to feel a personal acquaintance with Plutarch, and most readers will feel also a real affection for him. It is so easy to imagine Plutarch living his quiet, busy life there in Chaeronea that it is a pleasure to know that he has never been forgotten there, and that in the little village church there is an ancient marble chair which is still called the " Chair of Plutarch."

The more we read of Plutarch, the more do we become impressed with his many-sided excellence, with the wide horizon of his interests, and with his great knowledge. Yet though he wrote on so many and such varied subjects, and though a certain Roman did call him the " Living Library," it would be incorrect to call Plutarch an encyclopaedic writer. There is nothing impersonal in his writings. His readers were just as clearly before him when he wrote as were his hearers when he lectured.

Plutarch's popularity has gone up and down to some extent all through the centuries. He has been sometimes almost forgotten, and again re-discovered. Since the beginning of the present century there has been a decided revival of interest in Plutarch which is most gratifying to all those who have given any attention to his works.

To many of his readers Plutarch has been primarily a teacher. Professor Goodwin of Harvard used to say that Plutarch was a better teacher of rhetoric than any modern, and a passage in General Gordon's journal written at Khartoum states that he would like to have Plutarch's Lives made a handbook for young officers, " worth far more," he says in the journal, " than any number of treatises on the Art of War." Most people who read much of Plutarch's essays will be inclined to agree with Gilbert Murray who says of Plutarch that he is " one of the most tactful and charming of writers, and one of the most loveable characters in antiquity."

We cannot agree with Plutarch in all that he says. The differences between his age and ours, between his point of view and ours, are differences that cannot be ignored, and the reader will find him sometimes disappointing, as well as often suggestive. The essays are by no means all of equal merit. No one who wrote as much as Plutarch did could be at his best all the time. Among the essays there are some that are dull and some that are thin.

Yet there is hardly one that does not contain some sentence that is suggestive, some passage worth reading, something to make you glad that you looked into that essay, even though you may consider it, as a whole, very poor.

The leisurely way in which Plutarch writes often gives to the reader a feeling of leisure which is very restful. And his unfailing cheerfulness, his keen sense of humor, the fact that he found the world such a good place to live in, makes him a very pleasant companion. Plutarch is not an author to be read in a hurry, and it is a mistake to read too much at a time. But nothing can be more delightful than an occasional hour with that devoted teacher, that gentleman and scholar, so genial, wise, and kindly, who lived and lectured and wrote in that dull little town of Chaeronea.

A FRIEND OF MARCUS AURELIUS [1]

In the year 1815 when Cardinal Mai discovered in the Imperial Library at Milan a palimpsest containing some of the letters of Marcus Aurelius and Fronto, great interest was felt in the discovery. The bare fact that such a collection of letters had once existed had been known before from chance references, but nothing was known in regard to the character of the correspondence. And of Fronto very little was known except that he had had a very high reputation in his own time, and that that reputation continued for at least three hundred years. It is not strange that people took it for granted that the correspondence between such a man and Marcus Aurelius must be of intense interest and historical importance. Great was the disappointment therefore when it was learned that that was not the case, that a large proportion of the letters were written when Marcus Aurelius was very young and are simply letters between a teacher and his boy pupil. Many of them are devoted to detailed discussions of the pupil's themes and would have been dull reading if the pupil had not been the one who he was. The disappointment felt by the editors in the character of the correspondence is reflected in the first edition, in which the work of editing was carelessly and hastily done. The same rather contemptuous attitude is seen also in many of the later criticisms and allusions to the work, and thus the reader of the criticisms gains little idea of the real value of this correspondence. That the letters are commonplace, no one would deny. But although they are commonplace, they are not unimportant, for they throw a light on the personality of Marcus Aurelius not to be gained from any other source. They are also of value for the glimpses they give into the life of the Antonine Age.

The main facts in the life of Marcus Aurelius are familiar to everyone, and all the places associated with his early life are well known to everyone who is familiar with the Rome of to-day. He

[1] This article was first published in the *Christian Science Monitor* of June 30, 1926, and permission has been given by the *Christian Science Publishing Society* for republication.

was born in his father's home on the Caelian Hill where the
ground rises so slightly that visitors to Rome sometimes say they
cannot find the hill, although they have seen some of the churches
on or near it.   After the death of his father which occurred when
the child was very young, Marcus Aurelius lived for a time with
his grandfather whose home was near the site where the church of
St. John Lateran now stands.   We learn however from a passage
in the *Meditations* that later on he returned to live with his
mother again in the villa on the Caelian.   Then came the adoption
by Antoninus Pius in the year 138, and after that his home was in
the Imperial residence on the Palatine, first with Hadrian and
then with Antoninus Pius.   It will be remembered that this adoption was in accordance with the wish of Hadrian who in bringing
it about chose not only his own successor, but his successor's successor also.   Hadrian seems to have known Marcus Aurelius from
his earliest years and to have had to a certain extent at least the
direction of his up-bringing.   Although the boy was still very
young, Hadrian had seen enough of him to estimate his ability and
character, and he knew what he was doing when he sought to
bring it about that Marcus Aurelius should eventually become
Emperor of Rome.   With Antoninus Pius also the child had always been acquainted, for Faustina the wife of Antoninus was his
father's sister, and that close friendship which continued as long
as Antoninus Pius lived had begun long before the adoption.   It
was through the adoption that Marcus Aurelius received the
name by which he is known to history.   The name originally given
to him was that of his mother's grandfather, Catilius Severus, and
this name after his father's death had been changed to Annius
Verus.

It is evident that Marcus Aurelius had had a very happy childhood, although not much can be learned about it.   He was about
seventeen when Fronto was appointed as his tutor, and the acquaintance between the two beginning at this time speedily developed into an intimate friendship which continued as long as
Fronto lived.   The association between them was so close and so
continuous that it would be impossible to write a biography of
Marcus Aurelius without constant reference to Fronto, and it
would be hardly possible to read a biography of Marcus Aurelius
without becoming interested in his teacher and friend.

Fronto went to Rome from North Africa, his birthplace being that ancient city which since the fourth century has been called Constantine. Although he was quite young when he went to Rome, he had already attained distinction in his native city, and in Rome his reputation increased very rapidly. In an age celebrated for famous lawyers he became one of the most famous, and he was considered a very brilliant orator. He was also a profound student of the Latin language, a great lover of literature and a celebrated literary critic. In the Age of the Antonines there was an educated, cultivated society in the Mediterranean countries, an intellectual society interested in the things of the mind. The flourishing schools, the abundance of books and the growth of public libraries contributed to making the period a time of culture and general intelligence. It was a time when liberal education was so common, when there was such widespread interest in liberal studies, that the attempt to brand everything intellectual as " high-brow " would have been inconceivable. The second century of our era, although it was not a creative age, was essentially an appreciative age. There were many scholars at the time, and there were many more people of scholarly tastes. Never has there been a time when there were more or better lecturers, or when lecturers had more intelligent, more critical, or more appreciative audiences, and nothing conduced more to giving a man influence and a high position in society than the reputation of being an able lecturer or public speaker. It was doubtless this reputation that first brought Fronto to the notice of those who were seeking a tutor for Marcus Aurelius. But he was chosen not simply for his reputation as speaker and writer, but also because of his high character and attractive personality.

If any of Fronto's speeches had survived, posterity would probably have had a higher opinion of his ability as a writer than that formed on the basis of the letters alone. But none of his other writings could have had the intimate personal interest that the letters have. In reading the letters we are plunged at once into the midst of the correspondence, for there is no reason to suppose that the earliest extant were the first ones written. There are some however that were probably written as early as the year 139.

In the collection of the extant letters there are seven books, five containing those which were written before the year 161 when

Marcus Aurelius became Emperor, and two books of those belonging to the later period. Many of the earliest letters were written when Marcus Aurelius was in the country and Fronto in Rome. Fronto's home was on the Esquiline near where the church of Santa Maria Maggiore now stands, and so not very far from the Imperial residence on the Palatine, and it is probable that when they were both in Rome he saw his pupil nearly every day. But Marcus Aurelius in his earlier years regularly spent July and August in the country, and in other months also he frequently went for a time to one of the villas. Thus the names of many of the villas that Marcus Aurelius loved become very familiar in reading the letters, and the remains of some of them can still be traced. The one at Lorium about twelve miles from Rome on the Via Aurelia is mentioned several times and the site of this has been determined, but the remains are very insignificant. At Lanuvium there are extensive remains of a very large villa which is believed to have been the one that belonged to the Antonines, and portrait busts of both Antoninus Pius and Marcus Aurelius were found here. The villa at Alsium on the coast of Etruria is mentioned several times also. So many of the villas are referred to in the letters that it is noticeable that there is no reference to the great Villa of Hadrian near Tivoli, although that continued to be used by the Imperial families at least as late as the time of Elagabulus (218–222 A.D.). But it was a very simple country life that both Antoninus Pius and Marcus Aurelius enjoyed, and not such luxury as that of the Villa Hadriani.

Many of these earliest letters of Marcus refer to his studies and the exercises he was writing, for he continued this work even in vacation. Some of the letters themselves read very much like exercises in composition. There is such an evident attempt to put into practice in a real letter the rules which he had been taught in regard to epistolary style. Several letters seem to be continuing a talk between the boy and his teacher, and some of Fronto's have comments on exercises which Marcus had written. One thing which Fronto considered of primary importance in both speaking and writing was care in the choice of words, and in regard to this he has much to say. The first letter in the collection, written in the year 139 probably, is several pages long and entirely on that subject. He says that in some matters a man may pretend to know more than he does, may really seem to know more than he does know, but that in the use of words no pretence is possible. He thinks that Marcus is not always as careful as he ought to be, that he sometimes fails to notice the difference, the fine distinction, that the change of a single letter may make, and to illustrate this he discusses the difference between *pelluere* and *colluere*, words for which dictionaries give the same English equivalents. He urges Marcus to remember that one great difference between an average speaker and a real orator is that the former is satisfied with good words for expressing any thought, but the latter is not content with words that are merely good, if there are any better ones to be found. In a letter written after Marcus Aurelius held the title of Caesar, he implores the young man " for pity's sake," *miserere*, to strike out one word from a speech and never use it again. Marcus had made the blunder of saying *dictio* when he should have said *oratio*. Fronto criticizes his pupil also for not giving sufficient care in his writing to the order of words in a sentence. Aulus Gellius tells a story which is a good illustration of Fronto's deep interest in words for their own sake, in their exact meaning and history. On one occasion when he was busily engaged with some architects who were submitting plans for new baths which Fronto intended to have built, someone who was present happened to use a rather colloquial expression, *praeterpropter*, meaning " thereabout," and another objected to the word on the ground that it was a vulgarism. Thereupon Fronto dropped the business with the architects to discuss this word which he claimed was perfectly good Latin. He cited various authors who had used it, sent for a copy of Ennius and read to the company a passage in which *praeterpropter* is used, and continued his defence of the word until the discomfited purist fled, saying that he would discuss the matter with Fronto alone and at another time. While this conversation went on the architects waited, with how much impatience at the interruption is not told. It should be noticed that Fronto with all the emphasis he puts on the importance of the choice of words, at the same time warns his pupil against becoming pedantic. " Avoid the commonplace " is a good principle to a certain extent, but it should not be carried to excess, for a style in which there is a constant and evident attempt to avoid the commonplace becomes very wearisome. He tells Marcus that common words should always be chosen rather than the unusual, unless the unusual are really the more expressive. Fronto's system may sometimes seem a little artificial, but he had some very good ideas.

In some of the letters of Marcus we find replies to Fronto's criticisms. In one of these Marcus congratulates himself on having a teacher who is not afraid to speak the truth, and adds that from Fronto he has learned to hear the truth as well as to speak it. He refers also to the great difficulty of speaking the truth, that is, making one's statements so absolutely accurate that they are not open to any misinterpretation. "This matter of speaking the truth," he says, "is very difficult for both Gods and men." These remarks on speaking the truth show the appropriateness of Hadrian's play on the name Verus which the little boy received after the death of his father. At that time Hadrian often used the superlative and called the child *Verissimus*, and Verissimus is a name which would be very appropriate for that portrait of the young Marcus Aurelius which is now in the Capitoline Museum.

Although Marcus could accept criticism, he had opinions of his own and when he disagreed with his teacher he did not hesitate to say so. In one letter he says that the subject for a theme that Fronto had sent him was very improbable, and that it would take longer to make the situation seem credible than it would to write upon it, and he wished that Fronto would send him such a subject as he had asked for.

Some of the remarks which Marcus Aurelius makes in these earlier letters both on his own writing and on some of the authors he is reading are of interest. He did not care for Horace and says to Fronto in one letter, " Please don't remind me of Horace. He is as dead to me as Pollio." The reference is probably to Asinius Pollio, one of the contemporaries of Horace who in his own time had a high reputation as a poet, and also as an orator and historian, but of whose works nothing has survived. Much may be learned of him however from other writers, and the reference to him in this letter is significant because it indicates that Pollio's reputation which had been so great in the Augustan Age had not survived even to the middle of the second century. In one letter Marcus Aurelius says that he is indebted to Fronto for all the literature that he will ever know. In another he says that he is as far from Greek literature as his native Caelian Hill is from the land of Greece, and he calls himself for that reason " almost a living barbarian " (*paene opicum animantem*). Although Marcus refers to his knowledge of Greek as being so slight, it is to be noticed that when Fronto wrote a letter in Greek to the mother of Marcus Aurelius, he asked Marcus to read it himself before giving it to his mother, and correct any mistakes that he found. " For you are fresher in Greek than I am, and I should not like to have your mother look down on me as an ignoramus."

There are references in several letters to the verses that Marcus Aurelius wrote. Practice in verse-writing was regularly given in all Roman schools, not with the expectation of making poets, but as a useful exercise in gaining command of language, and Marcus Aurelius like all other students had such practice. In one letter he says that he is sending some of his verses to Fronto, but asks him not to let anyone see them. This desire that no one but Fronto should see these verses recalls a remark of Tacitus in regard to the poetry written by famous men. It is well known that Cicero's poetry was received with ridicule at the time and continued to be ridiculed, and Tacitus, referring to that fact, says that Caesar and Brutus also wrote poetry, but they were more fortunate than Cicero because fewer people knew they had done it. It is quite possible that Marcus Aurelius had read that remark of Tacitus. Fronto also refers several times to the verses of Marcus Aurelius and his desire that no one should see them. In one case he assures him that the package in which he is returning some of his verses has been done up so securely that no one can open it. He has sewed it up with strong thread, and then sealed the thread. Fronto also says that one of his other boys complained that Marcus read his hexameters so rapidly that no one else could commit them to memory. This is rather significant, because it implies that anyone might be expected to memorize a poem on a single hearing, if it were only read with a reasonable degree of slowness.

There is an interesting letter referring to the first speech which Marcus Aurelius made in the Senate. This was soon after he had been appointed Caesar, and in accordance with custom he had to make in the presence of the entire Senate a speech of thanks to the Emperor for conferring the title upon him. This was no slight ordeal for a boy of eighteen, and Marcus was working hard over it when he wrote to Fronto, " This Caesar-speech of mine is gripping me with hooked talons. Now I am learning how much work it is to round out and put into shape even a few lines. At last I am learning what it means to take time in writing." This last probably refers to advice which Fronto had often given him, to write slowly when he was composing, to take time for it. Marcus says that he had become so discouraged by his lack of success in composing the Caesar-speech that he had tried writing Greek " to see if he could do any better in the language that he did not know than in the one that he did know." Fronto also was a little nervous about the Caesar-speech, but it seems to have been a great success. Fronto evidently felt his responsibility as a teacher very deeply, and he says in one letter that his anxiety to have his pupil make good progress is keeping him awake nights. In another he says that he is growing young again because Marcus is advancing so rapidly.

In reading some of the letters of this eager young student of the second century we can hardly help regretting that he too could not have had the joy of study in Athens, as so many young Romans had both in that century and earlier, that he too could not have had some of the delightful student life in Greece which is described so vividly by Aulus Gellius who was one of his contemporaries and about his own age. But those who decided the matter were convinced that the future Roman Emperor should be educated in Rome.

Besides these letters which refer especially to the studies of Marcus Aurelius there are others which tell of the various little things that he was doing from day to day, and sometimes the two subjects are combined, as when he gives his program for an entire day. These are simply pleasant, chatty, commonplace letters, not of the slightest importance in themselves, but of interest for the very reason that they are so commonplace. In one of them we find the well known story of the encounter with the shepherds. One day when Marcus Aurelius and some companions were riding in the Campagna they happened to pass a great flock of sheep, and Marcus heard one of the shepherds say to the other, " We must look out for those horsemen; they will probably try to steal some sheep." Thereupon the youngster put spurs to his horse and rode straight at the flock. We can imagine the scampering of the sheep, and one of the shepherds who was even more frightened than the sheep threw his crook at the riders. The crook however did not hit the boy, but it did hit the innocent man who was riding with him, and in reading the letter you can almost hear the boy's chuckles.

In a letter written from one of the villas to which they had just gone Marcus says that on the way to the villa they had turned aside from the highroad to visit an ancient city, a very small place, *minutulum*, but very interesting for its antiquities, " both buildings and sacred ceremonies beyond number." This town was Anagni, and Marcus says that it did not have a corner, *nullus angulus*, where there was not chapel, or shrine, or temple. He also saw many books written on linen referring to sacred things. When they went out of the town he noticed on the gate an inscription of three words, *Flamen sume samentum.* This inscription evidently called upon the priest to put on something, but no one of the party had ever seen the word *samentum* before, and Marcus asked one of the townspeople what it meant. He was told that *samentum* was not a Latin word, but Hernican, and that it signified the pelt of the victim which the priest drew over his pointed cap when he entered the city. Marcus goes on to say that they learned many other things about Anagni which they were interested to know. It is to be regretted that Marcus did not relate these " many other things " and tell us all that he learned of Anagni in that brief visit. This ancient Hernican town, much older than Rome, was of great importance in its earlier period, and its importance revived again in mediaeval times when it was a favorite papal residence. But in the Roman period it sank into insignificance, and of Anagni in the time of the Roman Empire little is known beyond what is told in this letter. At the present time the town is as insignificant as it was in the second century for it occupies only the acropolis of the ancient city. The trip to Anagni is still one of the interesting trips to take from Rome, but it is mediaeval remains that one sees there now for the most part, and little of what Marcus Aurelius saw except for the impressive old walls. It would have been very interesting if we could have had a detailed account of what he did see, and it is disappointing to have him break off his account of Anagni at this point to ask where Fronto has decided to go for his vacation, to say how he misses him and beg him to write often. But in this letter as in various others where some interesting subject is just touched upon and then dropped, we have to remember that these letters were written not for posterity, but to Fronto.

In another letter Marcus gives the complete program of one of his days in the country. First he studied from three o'clock in the morning until eight, when he made his daily formal call on the Emperor. Then came a hunting excursion and of this he says, " We did valiant deeds, for we *heard* that some boars had been taken, but we ourselves did not see them." In the afternoon after returning from the hunt, he spent two hours on the couch reading a speech of Cato on the " Property of Pulchra." Of this speech nothing is now known, and Marcus evidently thinks that Fronto was not familiar with it either, for he is sure that Fronto will send immediately to the Library of Apollo for the book. This will be of no use however, for Marcus himself has borrowed the copy from the Apollo Library. So he suggests that Fronto try the library in the palace of Tiberius where he can probably obtain the book by giving a *mancia* to the librarian. There are various little remarks in the letters referring to the public and semi-public libraries in Rome. After he had finished reading this speech Marcus did a little writing, but he was not at all satisfied with it, and says that it was " such wretched stuff that it ought to be dedicated to the deities of fire or water." Then he says that he has taken cold and is going to bed, and considering that he began his day at three o'clock in the morning, the reader thinks that it is about time. Marcus closes this letter by telling Fronto how he longs to see him, " even more, I dare to say it, even more than I long to see Rome itself."

In a letter to Fronto written in the summer vacation Marcus says, " I have not seen you for two years. Some people say that it has been only two months, but they count only days." Marcus was counting his own feelings. The two months were probably July and August, the months of Fronto's consulate, when Marcus Aurelius was generally in the country.

Another letter gives the program for an entire day. This time he says that he slept rather late, and so did not begin study until five o'clock. He first did a little writing, " not quite such wretched stuff as that of the day before." After a very light luncheon he went to the vineyard and worked hard at grape-picking. When he returned from the vineyard he studied a little and then had a chat with his little mother, as he calls her, *matercula mea*. Later on they had an informal supper in the oil-press room and were much entertained by listening to the peasants chaffing each other, and the day is concluded with the letter to Fronto. There are many references in the letters to the vintage season which make one think of the Festa dell'Uva of the present time.

In a letter to Fronto written from Naples Marcus says that nothing has happened worth writing about, and then proceeds to describe the climate of Naples which he says is pleasant but violently variable, *vehementer varium.* " Every few minutes it changes and becomes colder, or warmer, or rougher. At midnight it is mild as at Laurentum; at cockcrow, it is chilly as at Lanuvium. After that until sunrise it is cold, very much like Algidus. During the forenoon it is sunny as at Tusculum, followed by a noon as fiercely hot as at Puteoli. But after sunset it is more moderate, something like Tivoli; and this continues until midnight," where the description began.

There is a rather amusing letter which Marcus Aurelius wrote from Baiae one summer. Fronto always thought that Marcus did not sleep enough and often remonstrated with him about it, and this letter is in reply to a very long one which Fronto had written him on the advantages of sleep. Fronto had given his pupil training in writing on both sides of a question, taking first one side and then the other. So in reply to this letter of Fronto Marcus writes that there is much to be said against sleep. Take the case of Ulysses for instance, and here he quotes verse after verse from the Odyssey. He would not have taken twenty years to return home after the Trojan War, and had all the other adventures and disasters which make up the story of the Odyssey, if he had not gone to sleep at such critical times. He quotes a verse of Homer also in praise of Agamemnon,

None might see the godlike Agamemnon sleeping;

and another verse,

No counsellor should sleep the whole night long.

Then referring to Fronto's remark that it was from sleep and a dream that the poet Ennius received his first inspiration to write,

Marcus says that if Ennius had kept on sleeping, he would never have told the dream. The close of the letter says that he has been writing all this in the evening and now it is time to go to sleep. We have also the reply to this letter. Fronto did not think much of it, and he implies that Marcus must have been very sleepy when he wrote it. He rather grudgingly commends the translations from Homer, but as to the remark made about Ennius, that he could not have told his dream if he had stayed asleep, he thinks that is really too flat. Finally Fronto says, "Why do you call me master, when the one thing that I especially want you to learn, to take sleep enough, I have never succeeded in teaching you?"

Various contemporaries of Marcus Aurelius of whom we know from other sources are mentioned in the letters. One of the most interesting of these is the Greek Herodes Atticus who was a very prominent figure in the Antonine Age. Herodes was an intense lover of his native Greece, and was passionately fond of Greek literature and Greek art. Aulus Gellius who knew him well speaks of his being renowned both for personal charm and for true Greek eloquence, and in another passage he says that Herodes in the use of the Greek language surpassed all the men of his time in "distinction, fluency, and elegance of diction." It is impossible for posterity to form any opinion of Herodes as an author, for although he wrote much, none of his writings are extant, unless it be one declamation the authorship of which is disputed. But what has kept his name in constant evidence both in Rome and in Athens are the buildings that he erected. He was a very wealthy man and a benefactor to various cities in both Greece and Italy. To Athens he gave a marble stadium on the site of which the modern stadium has been erected, and of which Pausanias says that in building it most of the marble in the quarries on Pentelicus was exhausted, and that it was "wonderful to see, though not so impressive to hear of." He also gave to Athens the Odeum or Music Hall of which remains are still to be seen. Of these two monuments both of which were in memory of his wife, Regilla, Philostratos the author of a life of Herodes says that they were "such as existed nowhere else in the Roman Empire." But with all that Herodes accomplished, he had to leave undone something that he had especially desired to achieve, to cut a canal through the Isthmus of Corinth. According to his biographer he felt that he had done nothing because he had not accomplished this, but it was not until seventeen centuries after his death that that plan was finally carried out.

The buildings of Herodes near Rome of which remains may still be seen are the tomb of his wife Regilla, who was a Roman, and a small temple. These two buildings are near the Via Appia Pignatelli and are well worth the little excursion to see them. The tomb is a charming little building, and it is no less picturesque because it now stands in a farmyard. It is of brick in two colors, yellow and dark red, and the combination of the two is very effective. This tomb is now called the *Tempio del Dio Redicolo,* but no reason can be found for that name and it is not known when it began to be used.

The temple also was erected after the death of Regilla in the year 161. It is a small tetrastyle temple which stands near the Bosco Sacro. It was made a church in the mediaeval period and is still known as the church of S. Urbano. In the transformation from a Pagan temple to a Christian church the interior was only slightly altered, and on the barrel vault there are still preserved traces of the ancient stucco decoration. There are also some interesting frescoes of the year 1011 illustrating the lives of S. Urbano and other saints which are of importance in the art of that period. To what deity the temple was dedicated is not absolutely certain, but it is believed that a statue of Annia Regilla stood in it originally.

Although Herodes Atticus was very philanthropic and very generous, although his biographer says that no man ever used wealth to better purpose, that he " laid up the treasures of his riches in the hearts of those who shared them with him," he seems to have had a most extraordinary faculty for making enemies. He roused great antagonism among the Athenians and they made such serious charges against him that he was brought to trial in Rome. The exact date of this trial is not known, but it was not earlier than the year 140 and not later than 143. The first letter in the correspondence in which Herodes is mentioned is one which Marcus Aurelius wrote to Fronto in regard to the trial. Fronto had been retained by the prosecution, and Marcus Aurelius who knew Herodes personally and believed that he was innocent of the charges made against him, was afraid that injustice might be done him through Fronto's eloquence. He evidently thought that it was very unfortunate for Herodes Atticus that the most convincing pleader in the Roman law-courts was on the side of the prosecution. Marcus Aurelius was quite young at the time and the letter is very modest in tone, but he feels that he must write as he does in regard to this matter even at the risk of Fronto's thinking that he is a bold little boy, *audax puerulum*. The style of this letter is to be noticed because it is so simple and direct. He goes straight to the point here, and there is none of the conscious attempt at style which is seen in some of the other letters of this period. Although the tone is so modest, yet this letter is not at all from the pupil writing to his tutor, as most of the others of this period are. It is from Caesar writing to a lawyer. There are several letters on this subject between the two, but they were all written before the trial took place, and so nothing about the result is learned from the correspondence. But since Herodes was appointed consul very soon afterwards, it is evident that he was honorably acquitted. One little remark of Fronto indicates the uncomplimentary language that might sometimes be used in a Roman law-court. In referring to the speech which he intends to make, he says, " Even if I should happen to call Herodes an ' ignorant greekling,' that will not be fatal." Whether Fronto actually used that expression or not, we do not know, but it is certain that he and Herodes afterwards became very good friends, and Fronto in a later letter says that Marcus Aurelius was unusually successful in bringing it about that his friends should like each other. Later on Herodes became one of the tutors of Marcus Aurelius and the one with whom he had his most satisfactory study of Greek. Although Marcus Aurelius claimed to know very little Greek, yet it was the Greek language that he used in writing his *Meditations,* and that indicates that Herodes Atticus had been an excellent teacher.

The letters shows that Fronto was on intimate terms with the whole Imperial family. He says that for Hadrian he had had great admiration, but that it would have seemed presumptuous to feel affection for him. But for Antoninus Pius he had deep affection as well as unbounded admiration, and he was constantly urging Marcus in his younger days to become a successor worthy of his father. He refers occasionally also to the devotion that Marcus himself felt for his father and which was so beautifully expressed many years later in the *Meditations*. It may be noticed that two letters that Fronto wrote to Antoninus Pius are among the best that Fronto ever wrote.

Fronto also had great admiration for the mother of Marcus Aurelius, Domitia Lucilla, and occasionally wrote to her and greetings both to her and from her are very frequent in the correspondence. One of the letters of Fronto was written for Domitia's birthday in the year 143. Domitia had sent out invitations for a birthday reception, and Fronto writes a very elaborate letter saying that he is very glad that his wife can accept the invitation, and expressing most polite regrets that because of official engagements it is impossible for him to go himself. This letter is rather excessively polite, so much so that it makes the reader wonder a little whether he really felt the regret that he expresses in such an elaborate form, or whether he was glad to have such a good excuse for not going. The sending of birthday greetings to friends was a very prevalent custom in the Antonine Age and there are many other such letters in the correspondence. In one of these Marcus Aurelius says that this yearly prayer of his for Fronto grows more and more comprehensive as the years go on and the duration of the friendship increases.

New Year's greetings were very common also and there are examples of these. In one such letter Fronto says to Marcus, " May the New Year be happy and prosperous both for yourself and for all who are dear to you." Fronto adds that he cannot go to the New Year reception at the Imperial palace because he is not well and fears the crowd and crush, *turba et impressio.* We have also the reply of Marcus Aurelius written after the reception was over in which he sends the " Season's Greetings " and tells Fronto that he is glad that he avoided the crowd and that Grace, Fronto's wife, did his part for him. He adds that the ceremony is to be repeated on a quieter scale day after tomorrow, and apparently hopes that Fronto may be able to go to the second and less crowded occasion.

Marcus Aurelius was married when he was quite young. As to the exact date historians disagree, but it was probably not far from the year 145. All the evidence that can be gathered goes to show that the marriage was in reality a very happy one, although posterity unfortunately has been led to believe the contrary because of scandalous tales related by a muck-raking biographer of a much later period. The unfortunate Faustina has been harshly judged, for in all times the public is ready to believe scandal without asking for proof. But no one could really study the evidence in this case without becoming convinced that the infamous stories that were circulated about Faustina in later times were wholly false. Someone has said that Faustina's worst fault was that she did not like her husband's friends. It is very possible that there were some of them whom she did not like. Faustina was a very beautiful vivacious young woman, but there is no evidence that she had any special intellectual interests, as the mother of Marcus Aurelius did have, and she probably did not care a straw for Stoic philosophy. And if she did not find anything really thrilling, or even congenial, in the conversation of some of the fusty old philosophers, as she may have thought of them, who came to see her husband, it is not to be wondered at. It is quite possible too that some of them did not like her, and thought that gaiety of manner indicated immorality, and that vivaciousness was a symptom of vice. But however that may be, the worst stories about Faustina were not invented until years after her death, and after Commodus had shown himself such a monster that people wanted to believe that he had had a bad mother.

The wife and children of Marcus Aurelius were very dear to Fronto and there are frequent references to them all through the correspondence. In several letters Marcus Aurelius refers to a baby daughter as "my little lady," *domnula mea,* and Fronto uses the same word when he sends messages and kisses to the little ladies. In one of the letters the reference is to a little lady only a few months old. Of another baby not more than six months old he writes, "She is such a serious old-fashioned little lady! When I want to kiss her little hands or her little feet, she draws them away." There is a delightful letter in which Fronto writes to Marcus Aurelius of going to see his twin babies who were at the time in the villa at Lorium, and he says that it was well worth the long ride over a bad road to see those chicks.

Just when Marcus Aurelius began to take more interest in philosophy than in literary studies, whether the change came rather suddenly or very gradually, cannot be determined. Some of his earliest teachers were Stoics and the boy became to some extent imbued with their ideas at a very early age. When he was only twelve years old he played at being a philosopher, and used to wear a rough cloak and sleep on the ground, until his mother protested. But long before Fronto became his tutor he had learned that philosophy does not consist in sleeping on the ground. He probably never lost the interest in philosophy which he began to feel so early in his life, but it is also probable that he never talked much about it to Fronto, for that was the one subject on which Fronto could neither sympathize with him, nor understand him. To Fronto therefore the change seemed very sudden, much more sudden probably than it really was, and his dismay when he learned how intense was the interest of Marcus Aurelius in philosophy is both amusing and pathetic. It is a little surprising to find that Fronto attributed this change of interest on the part of his pupil to a dislike of work. He said that Marcus was just like all other young people, he wanted an easy subject. Fronto was never able to comprehend the intense interest in philosophy which Marcus Aurelius felt. It was the one subject on which they could never get together, and Fronto could not refrain from occasionally jeering at philosophers, " those wonderful men who tell us that the wise man can be happy under any circumstances, that the wise man can be happy even when suffering torture." Fronto scornfully remarks that however happy a wise man might be under torture, he could not under torture compose a speech. To Marcus Aurelius, so intensely religious by nature, Stoic philosophy was religion in all that the word implies. To Fronto this philosophy which appealed to many of the best minds of his age, which has inspired some of the best minds of all ages, was never anything but a collection of absurd dogmas. It is noticeable that Marcus Aurelius in his letters to Fronto never mentions Stoic philosophy. Fronto could not comprehend the attitude of Marcus Aurelius, but Marcus Aurelius with his wonderful capacity for sympathy, with his ability to understand an attitude of mind absolutely at variance with his own, did understand Fronto. He knew that it was useless for them to try to get together on that subject, and so he wisely let it alone, and their friendship was never in any way lessened.

This correspondence between teacher and pupil, between two

friends one much older than the other, reveals Marcus Aurelius as
he was in boyhood and youth, sensitive, impressionable, enthusiastic, loving beauty and shrinking from grossness, admiring the
noble, detesting the mean and the petty, and altogether a very
lovable personality. A portrait bust now in the Capitoline Museum shows the same characteristics as those which are seen in
the letters.

We can understand Fronto's joy in seeing his pupil developing
and becoming such a man as his teacher had hoped he would be,
and it is pleasant to see that even after Marcus Aurelius had become Emperor the old relationship between the two hardly
changed. Fronto is still offering good advice and showing affectionate solicitude for his pupil's welfare. His letters on eloquence,
on the choice of words, on style in general in the use of the Latin
language, are even longer than in the earlier period. Some of
them are so long that one wonders how the Emperor in his busy
life ever found time to read them. Yet in almost every one there
are occasional juicy bits, though the letter as a whole may be
monotonous or even dull. Fronto is evidently watching with great
care every speech that Marcus Aurelius makes. In one letter he
says that he has not yet found anything artificial, or obscure, or
newfangled, or inflated in the speeches of the Emperor, but he
fears it. In another he criticises in detail one speech of Marcus
Aurelius, saying that parts of it were wonderfully fine, *mirifica*,
but that there were other passages that might be improved, and
he suggests various changes. In these later letters as well as in
the earlier Fronto has much to say on the importance of the language used, the importance of the choice of words. " Philosophy
will show you what to say, but it is eloquence that will teach you
how to say it." " The greater the thoughts, the more difficult it is
to clothe them in words, and much labor is needed to prevent
stately thoughts from being poorly clothed, unbecomingly dressed,
or even half-clad."

There is a very long letter from Fronto written to the Emperor
during the Parthian War after the Roman army had just suffered a serious defeat. The letter is one of attempted encouragement reminding the Emperor that Rome had always experienced
alternations of fortune, that Roman success had been gained
through defeat as well as by victory. He states this fact rather
well in one terse sentence, " Who is so unacquainted with the his-

tory of wars as not to know that the Roman people have attained supremacy *non minus cadendo quam caedendo?*" But Fronto could not stop with anything so concise as that. He has to go on and illustrate by one well known instance after another from all Roman history. Since Marcus Aurelius was quite as familiar with all the instances cited as Fronto himself was, it would not be strange if he deferred reading the greater part of this letter until the war was over. In this letter as in many of those written in the later period Fronto does not seem to know how to stop.

In many of the later letters Marcus Aurelius asks Fronto for advice in regard to his reading, and Fronto is always ready to give it. One reason, and probably the main reason, why Marcus Aurelius continued to ask such advice was that he knew how much it pleased Fronto to be asked. In one letter the Emperor had said that he has no time for reading now except by " snatches and by stealth," and Fronto in his reply urges him to be the " master of his duties " and take time for reading. That advice to master his duties is good, for the busy man is always in danger of letting his duties master him. In a very short letter the Emperor says that he is too busy to write but he wishes that Fronto would send him some extracts from Cicero's Letters, something that would be especially useful in improving his command of Latin. Fronto sends the extracts, but tells him that all of Cicero's letters ought to be read. Considering how overwhelmed with work Marcus Aurelius was, this advice to read Cicero's Letters entire was perhaps not altogether tactful. It is of some interest however to see that for language study Fronto considered the letters even more important than the orations.

Another letter of Fronto refers to the regret which Marcus Aurelius had expressed that so much that he had once learned had been gradually slipping away from him. There are many people who can sympathize with Marcus Aurelius in such regret, and may be interested in Fronto's reply that all success in life is the flowering and maturing of what has been learned. " Why regret the seed or the blossom after the fruit has matured? "

In the later correspondence just as in the earlier there are many family letters. Most of these and especially those of Marcus Aurelius are very short, but full of affection and with many references to his children.

Many letters in the collection refer to Fronto's health, so many that they seem monotonous to the reader. Fronto was never really well, and he was often ill. As soon as he recovered from one malady he was attacked by another. He suffered greatly from rheumatism for one thing, and in many letters there are references to attacks of that kind. In one of these he says that the Greeks gave to the backbone the name of sacred bone, and that Suetonius also called it the *spina sacra,* but for his part he would be perfectly willing to remain ignorant of the name, either Greek or Latin, of any bone in his anatomy, if he could only be free from pain in it. The letters of Marcus Aurelius when Fronto was ill are full of solicitude. He was always so anxious when Fronto was ill, and so relieved when he was better. In one of the earlier letters he says, "While you are down, my spirits will be down too. When you are standing on your feet again, my spirits will stand firm."

The letters on both sides are characterized by the rather excessive use, as it seems to most readers, of terms of endearment with many superlatives. That is especially the case in the earliest letters of Marcus Aurelius. The enthusiastic boy could not find superlatives enough to express his love and admiration for Fronto. He calls him the " sweetest of masters, most honored and rarest of men, my treasure, my delight, my joy." In another place Fronto is the " most affectionate, most delightful, and most eloquent of men." There is hardly a letter among the earliest ones of Marcus Aurelius which does not contain some such expressions, and they have been criticized as effusive and school-girlish by those who think that expressions of endearment are not in good form. The disgust that these terms of endearment have aroused in some of the English and American critics is really amusing, but the criticism is simply an illustration of our Anglo-Saxon repugnance to Latin impulsiveness. These terms would be effusive if they were used to any such extent in English letters, for they would not be natural. In this correspondence however the constant use of superlatives and reiterated terms of endearment is so natural that it should be considered spontaneity rather than effusiveness.

So many of Fronto's letters in the latter part of the correspondence are excessively long that they indicate that in these years he did not have much to do except write letters. There are other indications also in the latest letters that Fronto has become an old man. He takes especial delight in recalling the charming boyhood and attractive youth of Marcus Aurelius, and sometimes dwells on these to an extent that may have been a bore to the subject if he read it all. Marcus Aurelius had probably learned that in some of Fronto's letters there was much that he did not need to read. Fronto was something like the tutor of whom the poet Martial writes, in that he could not realize that his " beloved boy " as he used to call him had grown up. He continued to be just as solicitous for the Emperor as he had been for the schoolboy. Indeed his care sometimes seems a fussiness that would have been irritating to anyone else, but which Marcus Aurelius understood so perfectly that even if it was sometimes excessive, it caused him affectionate amusement instead of irritation. One thing that Fronto was especially worried about was that the Emperor worked too hard, and in that his anxiety was fully justified. Marcus Aurelius did work too hard and always had from the day of his becoming Emperor. He never had a day of leisure, and often admits that he is as he says, " worn out with labor," or as he says in another letter, " so tired that he can hardly breathe." Once when he was taking a few days in the country he wrote to Fronto that his holiday, so-called, was simply doing in the country the work of the city. He says that his cares are so pressing that he has respite from them only for a part of the night, and as we learn from other letters, it was often only a very small part. Fronto often urged him to take a few days for a real holiday, " but," he says, " if you have declared war on play, recreation, and pleasure, do at least sleep as a freeman ought to sleep." He begs the Emperor to observe the boundaries between day and night, and to emphasize this he wrote a parable, saying that in the beginning Jupiter divided day and night by the distinction of light and darkness, intending the former for work and the latter for rest. But after a time men began to use the night also for work, and then Jupiter proposed to put one of the other gods in charge of the night to prevent this. But he could not find anyone who was willing to undertake it. Neptune said that he could not, for it took all his time to keep the sea in order. Pluto said that it would be impossible for him, for Hades would break loose if he were not on duty there all the time. When Jupiter took the matter up with some of the other deities, he found that most of them wanted to be out nights themselves. Then Jupiter created Sleep, put him in charge of the night and rest, and " gave into his keeping the keys of men's eyes." In one letter written in the evening Fronto expresses the hope that the Emperor may sleep that night " without a thought that anything has to be done," but Marcus Aurelius during his whole reign had very few such nights.

Besides the correspondence between Fronto and Marcus Aurelius there are in the collection letters from both of them to other people. Some of these letters show that Fronto was one of the fortunate people who have a real genius for friendship, but the most interesting of the miscellaneous letters are those which he wrote to and received from Lucius Verus. One of these written to Lucius Verus when he was in Syria contains passages which would evidently have been of much historical interest, if they were not so mutilated as to make many parts unintelligible. Since Lucius Verus is one of the characters of whom history has had nothing good to say, it is significant that these letters give a very different idea of him from the opinion that is commonly held, and serve to throw doubt on many of the accusations against him. Among the letters of Marcus Aurelius to and from various people there are several that would be of great interest if they were genuine, but which recent scholarship has shown to be spurious. These include a pretended correspondence between Marcus Aurelius and Faustina at the time of the Cassius rebellion, but the letters, as is made evident by various facts, were probably not written earlier than the third century and perhaps even later. The Christian forgery which is found in the collection, and which pretends to be a letter from Marcus Aurelius to the Senate, was long ago recognized as spurious.

The last letter extant from Marcus Aurelius to Fronto was written in the year 165. This is a brief note of sympathy written when the Emperor had just heard of the death of Fronto's little grandson, a child about three years old. It is very short, for the Emperor was not well and was unable to write with his own hand. Fronto's reply is very long and very sad. He had lost his wife only a few months before the little grandson died, and he refers to that and to the many sorrows of that kind which he had suffered all through his life. He had had six children five of whom died very young, and in every case the child that died had been the only child. He says that he can " more easily believe that death transports us to those serene and delightful assemblies of souls where all joys are to be found," than he could believe that " human affairs are ruled either by no Providence, or by one that acts unfairly." But a little later he adds the universal truth that belief in the immortality of the soul does not heal a parent's grief. The heart-broken letter closes with the words, " If I were made of iron, I could not say more now."

When Fronto died is uncertain. No letter among those extant can be dated later than the year 166, and, as we have seen, the latest to Marcus Aurelius was written in 165. The whole tone of this last letter and the fact that his health was failing, makes it probable that he did not live very long after this. It is said that Marcus Aurelius conferred other high honors on Fronto, and also obtained permission from the Senate to have his statue placed in the Senate-house. While it is as the friend of Marcus Aurelius that Fronto is of special interest now, it should not be frogotten that he had been a man of national reputation and very prominent in the public life of Rome, and that it was on that ground, not because he was a personal friend of the Emperor, that his memory was honored in that way. It is to be hoped that Fronto's life was not prolonged much later than 166. The last years of the reign of Marcus Aurelius would have been very hard for him. They would have been passed in the midst of all the suffering in the City caused by the pestilence, in a constant state of apprehension caused by the war which was called the " War of All Nations," and in never-ending anxiety for Marcus Aurelius himself whose last years were spent in camp on the northern frontier. Fronto was an intense patriot, and could give no higher praise to anyone than to say that he was *patriae amantissimus*. The teacher and his pupil, the Emperor and his friend, were always in complete accord in their love and veneration for the Roman past, in their reverence for the heroes of old, in their respect for established traditions, and in their conviction that in faithfulness to these lay the strength of the Empire. While we cannot know just when Fronto died, there is one thing of which we can be sure, and that is that as long as he lived Marcus Aurelius never ceased to write to him. He says to himself in the *Meditations,* " Never say too often or write in a letter, ' I am too busy,' " and he was never too busy to write to Fronto, even when the letters had to be very short.

There are extant very few authentic letters of Marcus Aurelius written in the last ten or fifteen years of his life, so all the knowledge that we have of him in the last period is derived from other sources. It will be remembered that he was with the army on the Danube when he died in the year 180, and that he had gone there two years earlier. His last years were hard and sad, and in reading the *Meditations* one ought always to remember when and where and why they were written. It was in those last sad years when the cares of state were weighing heavily upon him, when after his valiant struggle to save the civilization of the past, he was beginning to question whether it could be saved. They were written in his tent at night when he was unable to sleep. And as to why they were written, it certainly was not with any intention of preaching or of teaching. This note-book, for that is all it is, was not written for other people to read. It was no more intended for posterity than were the letters to Fronto. It was to himself and for himself that he jotted down these thoughts, and it was probably by mere chance, a most fortunate chance, that the book was preserved. This note-book, commonly called " The Meditations of Marcus Aurelius," is something that will never cease to be read, and it has made Marcus Aurelius more real to thousands of people than any history or biography could have made him. It is intensely personal and it gives the reader a certain feeling of personal acquaintance with Marcus Aurelius, and yet the conception of him that is gained from this book alone is incomplete, and so it is not wholly correct. The thoughts, beautiful though they are, are tinged with a certain sadness which was not characteristic of Marcus Aurelius in his earlier years. That same sadness is seen in many of his later portraits. The portraits of Marcus Aurelius were so many that when he died they were to be seen in almost every house in Rome. More than a century later the author of a biography says, " Even to-day portraits of Marcus Aurelius stand in many a home among the household Gods." And now in the twentieth century we may say that even to-day portraits of Marcus Aurelius may be seen in every country that once formed a part of the Roman Empire. But although they are so many, there is hardly one that is really satisfactory as a portrait of Marcus Aurelius. In this respect they are very different from those of Antoninus Pius. The portraits of Antoninus Pius look as we should expect him to look. The man whom we see in the portrait is just the man of whom we read. But the portraits of Marcus Aurelius, the later ones at least, are not what we should expect. Perhaps they look as he looked, but they do not look as we should imagine him, they do not look as we want him to. They are so careworn, so tired. There are several that recall his own words, " so tired that he could hardly breathe."

Marcus Aurelius died in his tent after an illness of only a few days apparently, although he had long been far from well. According to the biographer he died *ridens res humanas*. That word *ridens* has sometimes been misinterpreted and translated *with derision*, but the word *ridens* does not generally imply derision and there is no reason for imputing that meaning to it here. The word signifies amusement rather than contempt. It means *laughing* and should be so rendered, or as one translator expresses it, " with a smile for the vanities of the world." The word recalls a letter of Fronto written nearly forty years before Marcus Aurelius died, in which he says, " Laugh, Caesar, and be happy." Marcus Aurelius for many years had not laughed as much as his old tutor would have wished, and there is a certain satisfaction in hoping that perhaps at the very end of his life he did reach the point where he could see something of the comedy as well as the tragedy of *res humanas*, where he could, to quote the words of the poet Masefield, where he could

Laugh and be proud to belong to the old proud pageant of man.

It is not necessary to reiterate what is perfectly evident, that this correspondence is not of value as literature. The comments in most histories of Latin literature that touch upon it at all are disparaging. It is said that the style is often poor, the subjects unimportant, and the Latin shows signs of decadence. That is all perfectly true. These letters have none of the raciness of Cicero's nor the polish of Pliny's, and will not bear comparison with either the one or the other. The letters of Marcus Aurelius, although they are the letters of a great man, are certainly not great letters. It is therefore surprising to find that Philostratos, a Greek critic and author of biographies who lived only about a generation later than Marcus Aurelius, ranks him among great letter-writers. Of course we do not know what letters of Marcus Aurelius may have been in existence in the early third century which are not extant now, but among those which are extant there is nothing to justify that opinion. But these letters are like many other writings in post-classical Latin in that whatever they lack in form is more than made up for by their human interest. However small the literary value, the biographical importance is great, and to anyone who reads the correspondence from that point of view, the criticism of the purist that the Latin is decadent, must seem rather petty. It is as a human document, not as a work of literature, that this correspondence should be read.

The first glimpse that we have of Marcus Aurelius is that little child, so earnest 'and so frank that Hadrian used to call him Verissimus instead of Verus. Then through the letters we may have glimpses of him all the way along. We see the merry boy who when he was riding in the Campagna and saw that the shepherds were afraid of him frightened them still more. We see the affectionate boy who writes so charmingly of his talks with his mother, and who when he wanted to write to his tutor from Naples one day had so little to say that he was forced to write about the weather. We see the enthusiastic young student, so interested in the antiquities of the old town of Anagni, keen in his reading, working hard at his writing, following his tutor's instructions to the best of his ability but not in any unthinking way, not lacking discrimination, having opinions of his own, and when he disagreed with his tutor never hesitating to say so. We see him a youth of eighteen struggling over his first speech in the Senate. Later on we see Marcus Aurelius in his home life, when almost every letter to Fronto has some reference to his wife and his children. These references are indeed very slight, but they are significant. Then come the latest letters in which we see the overburdened Emperor whose working day was often twenty hours instead of eight, but who could always even in his busiest days take time for a few lines to his old tutor.

After reading these letters we realize how incomplete is the conception of Marcus Aurelius which is received from the note-book alone. He himself says somewhere, " Live as on a mountain-top," and to the reader whose only knowledge of Marcus Aurelius is that gained from the note-book, he seems to do just that. He seems to be living on heights to which the average man could never attain. But the letters show that although he had reached the heights, he never ceased to be a man among men. To the reader of the note-book he seems to be especially a man of thought. He was that, but he was also a man of action. The reader of the note-book might think of Marcus Aurelius as a dreamer. The letters show that he was eminently practical. The reader of the note-book might think of Marcus Aurelius as a Stoic saint only. He was a Stoic saint, but he was also a Roman statesman and a Roman soldier. The reader of the note-book might think of Marcus Aurelius as solitary and perhaps inclined to avoid human companionship. The letters show that he was most companionable, that human sympathy was one of his outstanding qualities, that he was one of the kindest men that ever lived. It has been said of Marcus Aurelius that he belonged not to any single age, or country, or race, but to all humanity. That is very true, but the letters show that he was also very thoroughly Roman.

After reading the letters one can understand the universal love that was felt for Marcus Aurelius and the personal grief that his death brought to thousands of people. People of all ages loved him as if he belonged to them. The old men, so it was said, loved him as a son, the middle-aged as a brother, and the young people loved him as a father. Herodian, a Greek historian who was a boy when Marcus Aurelius died, says that at his death he left a longing for him in the hearts of living men, and an immortal memory. Herodian's prophecy has been fulfilled, for the memory that has been so vivid for more than seventeen hundred years will never die.

Fronto once said of Marcus Aurelius something with which posterity will always agree, that he was " an honor to his fatherland and to the Roman name." After reading the letters one likes to repeat that, *decus patriae et Romani nominis*. But we want also to add something to it and say of Marcus Aurelius what he himself said of Fronto, that he was " the friendliest of friends." *Amicorum amicissimus*, that is Marcus Aurelius as seen through the letters.

LIGHT READING FROM THE ROMAN EMPIRE

ONE of the authors of long ago in whom renewed interest has been aroused recently by the series entitled " Our Debt to Greece and Rome " is the African Apuleius who lived in the second century A.D. It may not be Latin authors to whom most people would turn when they want light reading, something for recreation only. But among the extant writings of the Roman Empire there is plenty of light reading to be found and even fiction, and the romance of Apuleius is unique. The story of the author's life, if told in detail, would read like a romance. An African of Greek descent and a Roman citizen by birth, he was not fully either Roman, Greek, or African, but a combination of all three. Although born in a Roman colony, he did not learn Latin until he went to Rome and acquired the language, as he says himself, " with grievous toil and no teacher." In his writings however it was the Latin language that he used, but the fact that it was not his native tongue is constantly apparent.

By profession Apuleius was a travelling lecturer, and lectures have never been more common or more frequented than they were in the second century. It was long before modern times that the idea of popular lectures and " university extension " originated. Apuleius was a keen student of human society, and his profession, which took him into all parts of the Roman world, gave him opportunities to see all varieties of society and every kind of life. One of his experiences would make good fiction if it were not actual fact. After an extensive tour he was staying for a time in Tripoli, one of those old African towns to which new interest has been given in recent years by the excavations which are still going on. Here he was the guest of a young man who had been one of his fellow-students in Athens and who was then living in Tripoli with his widowed mother. The tranquillity of the visit was suddenly interrupted by a suggestion made to Apuleius that he marry the widow! This proposal, which came from the son, struck Apuleius like a bomb. He had had no thought of marrying any-

one, and certainly not a widow old enough to be his mother. But
the son was insistent. Knowing that his mother had determined
to marry again, he wished to select the bridegroom. Many were
the arguments that he used in urging his young friend to accept the
position, but the most convincing one was the fact that the widow
was rich, for Apuleius had spent most of his inheritance in his
travels and was in desperate need of funds. Moreover she was
" a nice woman." Apuleius liked her, and after he had recovered
from the first shock, he said to himself, " Why not? " and thus
the marriage took place. At first all went well, but after a time
the son died, and then trouble began. The widow's brother and
other members of the family feared that the property would come
into the hands of Apuleius. To prevent this, they proceeded to
bring against him a formal accusation of being a magician and
using his black art to induce the widow to marry him. This was
a serious matter and Apuleius was summarily brought to trial.
The charge of the use of magic was quite as dangerous in the second century as the charge of witchcraft was in a later age, and
Apuleius, who had unbounded intellectual curiosity in many lines,
was undoubtedly interested in magic. The accusers thought that
they had an easy case, but the defendant, who had studied and
practised law, conducted his own defense and did it with consum-
mate skill. The speech which he made on this occasion is still
extant and some parts of it are very entertaining and may be ap-
propriately called light reading. Fortunately for him the accusers had weakened their case by adding to the serious charge of
the use of magic certain absurd accusations, such as using denti-
frice and owning a mirror. It was on the weak points that
Apuleius seized at once, and he held the accusers up to unsparing
ridicule. He had become a very effective and very popular public
speaker and he used all his skill in arousing merriment among the
judges, thus diverting their attention from the serious charge, and
in giving entertainment to the audience. It was a public trial and
quite as crowded as a similar trial might be to-day. The prisoner
at the bar, being his own advocate, discoursed in a free and easy
way on various topics that had nothing to do with the question
before the court. He talked about philosophy, poetry, and
the definition of poverty, the fact that it is not a man's birthplace
but his character that matters, about medicine, natural history,

science, and various other topics, while he skilfully avoided every point that he would have difficulty in meeting. The whole tone of the speech is both facetious and contemptuous, calculated to give the impression that the accusers were extremely and absurdly ignorant. But although he declared that their charges were based on stupid and malicious interpretations of his experiments in natural science, he avoided giving any explanation as to the nature of these experiments. In the second part of his defense Apuleius attacked the character of his accusers. Scandals of all kinds, which, whether they were facts or mere suspicions, might better have been left unknown, were dragged into publicity, and this part of the speech rivals newspaper accounts of some modern divorce trials. Some passages are indeed exceedingly unpleasant reading, but the speech is throughout so animated, the pictures that it presents are so clear, that the reader seems to be actually in the courtroom listening, rather than reading.

That Apuleius was acquitted in this trial, there can be little doubt. He had won the sympathy of the judges and the applause of the audience, and left the courtroom as a conquering hero. Yet he well knew that he had not met the serious part of the charges against him. He was and he continued to be interested in magic to an extent that would have been considered criminal by many of his contemporaries. People had been dazzled by his clever and brilliant defense, but he was not unaware that lurking suspicions might still exist which would grow stronger and stronger as time went on. He showed good judgment therefore when he decided to leave Tripoli and settle in Carthage.

Since the marriage of Apuleius and Pudentilla came about in the way in which it did, it is interesting to know that it seems to have been a happy marriage in spite of the disparity in their ages. Just what the difference was is uncertain, since the accusers declared that the widow was sixty at the time of her marriage, while Apuleius said that she was only forty. In referring to Pudentilla as a helpful wife, an ancient commentator remarked that she was " one of those noble Roman wives who held the lights while their husband's wrote." These words a later commentator took very literally and expressed sympathy for Pudentilla, saying that it must have been very tiring to " stand by her husband all night with a candle in each hand." (Light reading which was not so intended is sometimes found in comments made on classical authors.)

There are extant also extracts from other speeches of Apuleius some of which show his skill in the art of saying nothing in an effective way, an art on which the reputations of other popular speakers, both ancient and modern, have in some cases been founded.

In his own time it was as a public lecturer and a Platonic philosopher that Apuleius was best known, but to-day he is chiefly interesting as a story-teller, the author of the only Latin romance which has survived entire, and which the author of an English translation made in the sixteenth century characterized as " a pleasant and delectable tale." The story is told in the first person and relates the adventures of a young Greek, Lucius by name. Like some modern stories, it begins very abruptly, " I was going to Thessaly, the country from which my mother's people came, and I was going on business." Thus we are launched at once on the narrative, and the lively descriptions transport the reader into the Thessaly of the second century. Lucius is represented as being keenly interested in magic, and when he found himself actually in Thessaly, the country which was especially noted for powerful magicians, his excitement knew no bounds. In that land, he says, he " expected to see statues walk, to hear walls talk and oxen prophesy, and to behold oracles falling straight from heaven." He could hardly believe that anything was what it seemed to be, but thought that even the birds and trees must be men transformed. At first however there was nothing out of the ordinary, but adventures soon began.

This narrative includes many short stories. Some of the experiences which Lucius himself had make complete short stories, and many of the people whom he meets have stories to tell. They are all very vivid, and some of them, which seem to come straight from a tourist's note-book, may be records, to a certain extent at least, of experiences which the author had actually had in his travels. Others are wholly unreal and very fantastic, but most entertaining. There are all kinds of stories in the collection. Some are horrible, some are ludicrous, some are thrilling, and one is very beautiful. Even the horrible ones are in some cases so ludicrous that the horror does not horrify. Cruelty is depicted not infrequently, but the whole atmosphere is so unreal that such scenes are hardly revolting although some of them are certainly thrilling. In one of these " pleasant and delectable tales " a dead man by means of magic is brought back to life temporarily. Thereupon he sits up in his coffin and holds a heated discussion with his wife as to the cause of his death, and the remarks of his wife imply that that was just like him. The bystanders take sides and join in the discussion, some of them declaring that the wife was a wicked woman, while others were sure that the corpse had lied.

Another story tells of a man who was killed in the night by witches, and his travelling companion, who had witnessed it all and knew that he would be accused of the murder, tried to hang himself. But the rope broke and he fell on the body of the murdered man who immediately sat up and began to protest, not knowing that he had been killed.

There are several stories which may be accounts of actual occurrences one of which tells of the wife of an Imperial Procurator who disguised herself as a man, followed her husband into exile, and finally brought about his recall. Even the brigand who tells this story expresses great admiration for that "most saintly woman," although she had upset all his plans and caused his band to be broken up.

Stories of faithless wives and their lovers are not lacking, and the story of the Wicked Stepmother would need only very slight changes to convert it into a modern detective story. This is told in great detail, how the woman tried to poison her stepson, and how it was her own son instead who drank the poison, and the stepson was accused of being the murderer. Then follows a full account of the trial, and it looks as if the innocent young man would be convicted on the false statements of a guilty slave. But just as the voting of the judge was about to begin, an old physician arose and asked to give evidence. The speech of the old physician is given in full and is well worth reading. He tells how a slave of the stepmother came to him and asked for poison, giving a very improbable reason for wanting it. The physician therefore became suspicious and was unwilling to furnish the poison. But fearing that if he refused, the slave would get it elsewhere, he gave him a drug which was harmless but caused long continued uncon-

sciousness. When all this had been told in court, the trial was
adjourned, everybody hurried to the sepulcher, the coffin was
taken out, and the boy was found beginning to open his eyes. So
all ends happily, except for the wicked stepmother who was
exiled for life, and the wicked slave who was hung.

And among these stories, horrible, or ludicrous, or amusing, or
thrilling, there is one so exquisitely beautiful that it is one of the
gems of literature, a story by which poets and painters have been
inspired all through the ages. This is one of the cases where a part
is more famous than the whole, for many people are familiar with
the story of Cupid and Psyche who might not know even the
name of the author. That the story itself is one that had been
handed down by word of mouth for many generations, for centuries perhaps, there can be no doubt, and yet there is no trace of
it in either Greek or Latin literature until it appears in this late
period, and in a highly elaborate form. Later versions of the story
omit for the most part the sophisticated touches, all the burlesque
and the parody. But while some of the later versions are indeed
very beautiful, they are in some respects quite different from the
original, for the sophisticated touches are eminently characteristic of Apuleius. Making fun of the Olympian deities was very
common in the age when Apuleius wrote, and throughout the
whole story the Olympians are represented as being governed by
Roman law. Juno, for instance, does not dare to protect Psyche
because the Roman law forbids giving help to other people's runa-
way slaves without the master's consent. Psyche, in telling her sister how Cupid has sent her away, makes him use the Roman formula for divorce, *tibi res tuas habeto.* Venus declares that her son's
marriage is illegal, not meeting the conditions required by law, but
in the happy ending Jupiter assures her that the marriage shall
be made legitimate and quite in accordance with the *ius civile.* A
full attendance at the meeting of the gods which was called on this
occasion is secured by the proclamation that all absent members
would be heavily fined. The story ends with a wedding banquet
at which the gods were assigned places in order of rank, various
deities contributed to the delights of the occasion, and Vulcan
cooked the dinner. That was naturally Vulcan's contribution,
since it is Vulcan who, in one form or another, cooks all dinners.

In this story, as in the narrative as a whole, some of the minor

characters are well drawn, and one of these is the gossiping gull.
It is this loquacious bird, an inveterate talker and full of curiosity
about other people's concerns, who goes to Venus to tell her of her
son's love-affair, " lacerating his reputation." And the gull makes
Venus exceedingly angry too by repeating all the uncomplimentary remarks that she has heard, as she says, about Venus' whole
family.

In the first part of the story when the old king goes to consult
the oracle of Apollo, it is stated that Apollo, although he was a
Greek himself, gave his reply this time in Latin, " for the convenience of the author of the story." And kind old Pan makes a
remark that is very characteristic of Apuleius, " If I guess right,
and that is what wise men mean when they say *divination*."

Many learned writers have tried to make an allegory of this
charming story, believing that the names, Cupid and Psyche, indicated that intention on the part of the author. But if the two
had been called by any other names, or simply the beautiful
princess and the mysterious lover, instead of Psyche and Cupid, the
story would have been just as good. Allegorical interpretations
have been as varied as they are numerous, and the fact that those
who think they find allegory seldom agree on the exact meaning
shows how impossible it is to trace any consistent allegory in the
story as told by Apuleius. He himself probably never thought of
allegorical interpretation and that whole idea belongs to a later
age. The reader who would enjoy this tale as the author meant
it to be enjoyed, should not search for hidden meanings but simply
accept it as a fairy story, and one of the most delightful that was
ever told.

These stories in which the narrative abounds, told by one person after another whom Lucius meets, all come in naturally
enough, but any or all of them could be omitted without affecting
the main narrative. Going back now to this, we find that Lucius
meets all kinds of people in his journey through Thessaly, and
many of them are so clearly drawn that the reader does not forget
them although they flash on and off the screen like a moving
picture. We see doctors and merchants, farmers and bankers,
soldiers and housemaids, the great lady, the country laborer, and
the rich man who tries to conceal his wealth that he may not be
called upon to use any of it for the public good. The narrative

is characterized too by clever bits of satire which are thrown in here and there, sometimes unexpected, but always to the point. On reaching the city of Hypata Lucius was invited to be the guest of a man to whom he had brought a letter of introduction, and he was also most cordially received by an old friend of his mother, a woman very prominent in society. There is a full description of this woman's house which was marvelously beautiful and filled with works of art. Some of the sculpture was truly extraordinary, statues of dogs, for instance, so skilfully wrought that " their forefeet seemed to be running while their hindfeet were standing still," and clusters of grapes that seemed to be actually moving in the air. The account of a great dinner-party in this house is full of interest, with the description of the guests and the animated table conversation, some parts of which sound very modern. The stranger was assured by the people whose " home town " Hypata was that there was no other town equal to it. It was " the most interesting city in the world," like various modern cities.

Lucius had been warned by his mother's friend that the wife of the man in whose house he was staying was a powerful witch and that he must be constantly on his guard against her. Little did the friend suspect the joy that this information gave the young man. Witchcraft was his chief interest in Thessaly, and to find that he was actually living in the house with a real witch was better luck than he could have hoped for. He began at once to make love to the maid, thinking that that would be the most effective way of learning about the mistress. In this he was so successful that after a few days the maid took him to a room where through a chink in the door he watched the woman transform herself into an owl. The transformation, which was effected by the use of an ointment, seemed so simple that Lucius was eager to try it, and as Fotis, the maid, knew where her mistress kept her ointments, she promised to bring him some the next evening after the mistress had again become an owl and flown away. The maid kept her promise, but while she was waiting in the next room expecting to see a bird fly out of the window, she was horrified when instead of that she heard a donkey bray. She had made a mistake in the ointment! Fotis' profuse apologies were of little comfort to Lucius who longed for a human voice to tell her what he thought of her. He refrained however from his natural desire to kick her, because she was the only one who knew who he was and could help him. Fotis assured him that the re-transformation into a human being would be very simple, for all that he needed was to eat roses, and she promised to bring him some early the next morning. With that promise poor Lucius had to resign himself to being led to the stable for the remainder of the night. He thought that in the stable he would at least be welcomed by his own horse, but to his surprise that ungrateful beast did not recognize him and drove him away from the manger. Lucius tried to keep up his courage by thinking of the morning when he would be restored to human form, but long before daylight disaster came upon him. A band of robbers broke into the house and carried off everything they could lay their hands on, including the ass on whose ill-fated back they loaded their plunder. As Lucius was being driven through the streets with his heavy load it occurred to him that since he was a Roman citizen, he had the right to appeal to Caesar, and he tried to cry out, " Oh Caesar! " But all that he could utter was the " Oh! Oh-o-o! Oh-o-o-o! Oh-o-o-o-o! " much prolonged and many times repeated, and anyone who has ever heard a donkey bray can imagine just how it sounded.

In his life as an ass one of Lucius' difficulties was in learning to eat hay because, as he says, he had never been accustomed to it. His one comfort in his misfortune was in the length of his ears. He had always liked to hear what people were saying, especially when it was not for him that their remarks were intended, and now his ears were so long that he could hear people talking who were a long distance away and never suspected that he was listening.

All through the narrative there are admirable bits of description. For instance, the wild mountainous region where the robbers' cave was is brought before the reader as clearly as in a picture. We feel that the author must have actually seen the place which he describes. Soon after Lucius and the men who stole him came to the cave, another group of robbers, members of the same band, arrived. This second group had not been as fortunate as those who had stolen Lucius, and they give long accounts of their disappointments. In one case the owner of the house which they had entered had the effrontery to attack the robbers and shout for help, " the vile wretch! " Another house on their list was one where an old woman lived alone, and for that they thought one man would be enough. But he very carelessly neglected to strangle the old woman before he began to gather up her possessions, and that aged sinner by some pretence persuaded the robber to look out of the window, and when he leaned over the sill, she pushed him out! It must have been a feeble push, the narrator says, " but it was so sudden! " The account of the robber disguised as a bear makes a good story, but the bear's skin was his undoing. Altogether this group had had such bad luck that they had become pessimistic and were convinced that human beings are treacherous and that good faith is not to be found anywhere in this mortal life.

The next episode of interest is the arrival at the cave of a beautiful young girl whom the robbers had kidnapped and intended to hold for ransom. When the girl, left in charge of the old woman who served as the robbers' cook, was weeping and lamenting, the old woman tried to comfort her and said that she would tell her " a pretty story, an old wives' tale." Then follows the long story of Cupid and Psyche told in language often elaborate, sometimes poetic, and in many passages exquisitely beautiful. The atmosphere throughout the story is so unreal, and the reader is taken so far away from the main narrative, that it is rather a jolt when the ass remarks, " Such was the story told by that crazy, drunken old woman." That the story itself should have been told by an old hag in a robbers' cave might not have seemed as incongruous to the contemporaries of Apuleius as it does to the reader of today, for it was doubtless such a well known story that it may often have been repeated by ignorant old women. But the language which Apuleius ascribes to this old woman is a startling incongruity in the mouth of an old hag whose natural speech seems to be Billingsgate.

Then came a day when the girl and the ass were left in the cave with only the old woman to watch them and they tried to escape. The ass broke loose first, and when the old woman caught him by the halter, she showed " an audacity unsuitable to her age and sex." But when the girl snatched the halter out of the old woman's hand and mounted the ass, that was a " deed worthy of a man." Off they went together and the girl's promises to the ass, if he succeeds in carrying her home, are in Apuleius' most elaborate vein. Not only should he be most carefully tended, adorned with her own necklaces and fed with dainties from her own hand, but he should march in processions as a hero. The story of the rescue was to be represented in a wall-painting where many people would see and admire it, and the whole history would be recorded by learned men and handed down to posterity. But these fine promises were of no avail, for, owing to the girl's inability to understand the ass, the fugitives were caught. When they came to a place where three roads met, the girl naturally wanted to take the one which led to her home. But the ass, whose long ears had overheard the robbers' plans, knew that that was the road which they had taken, and that the only chance to escape them was to go in another direction for a time. So while the ass was trying to take one road and the girl was trying to force him to take another, they stood there " like people disputing about the right of way," until the robbers came upon them and they were driven back to the cave again. The robbers were so furious at the attempted escape that they planned to kill both girl and donkey the next day, and Lucius began to weep " for the corpse that he would be on the morrow." But at this point two new characters appear. One of the robbers who had stayed behind at Hypata arrived and reported that there was no danger of the band ever being suspected of that robbery because all suspicion had fallen on a certain young man who had been staying in the house, but had mysteriously disappeared on the night of the robbery and was never seen again. Poor Lucius! That he should be accused of being guilty of a robbery in which he himself had been an unhappy part of the booty seemed to him the climax of his misfortunes. He tried to cry out that he did not do it, but although that needed only two words, *Non feci*, and he could utter the first, the second was too much for him. He could only keep repeating " No-o-n, No-o-o-n, No-o-o-n," and those who heard him little realized what it meant, but thought it was only the ordinary braying of an ass.

There is also a new robber, introduced by the one just returned from Hypata, who wants to join the band. This man, claiming that his reputation is world-wide, can tell bigger stories than any of the others, stories of which one commentator remarks that they are enough to make anyone want to be a brigand. He aroused such enthusiasm that he was elected chief of the band, and when he proposed to sell the girl as a slave, they all agreed. To the great surprise of the ass, the girl manifested no terror at this fate. She even smiled, and when Lucius saw her accept a surreptitious kiss from the new robber, he was scandalized. This girl was evidently not what he had supposed her to be, and " naturally," as he says, he began to revile the whole sex, and thus " the reputation of all womankind hung upon the judgment of an ass." Those who have read much of Apuleius could hardly fail to hear him mutter under his breath as he wrote that, " And it was not the only time." The action is rapid in the remainder of this episode. As the reader may have guessed, Charité had recognized the new robber, for he was her betrothed who had come to rescue her. He told the band that his skill as a cook was as marvelous as his success as a brigand, and proceeded to prepare a sumptuous meal. He then acted as waiter, serving wine in such abundance that one after another the robbers fell on the floor unconscious. When they were all in that condition he bound them fast with cords, put the girl on the donkey's back, and they left the cave. Then follows the joyful arrival at the girl's home, the execution of the entire band of robbers, and the wedding. Charité fulfilled her promises to Lucius by giving him everything that an ass could possibly want, and he was sent off to the country where he was to have nothing to do but enjoy life. At this point we take leave of Charité and her husband, supposing that they will " live happily ever after."

Lucius too trotted off happily, thinking that in the country he would surely find the roses that would restore him to human form. But again he was doomed to disappointment. The man into whose charge he was given was kind enough, but unfortunately he had a wife, and the wife would have no idle donkeys about. She not only made him work for herself but she hired him out to the neighbors, and so between heavy work and cruel treatment poor Lucius had a harder time than ever before. From this situation he was rescued by some servants of Charité's family, and they have a long story to tell which comes as a surprise to the reader. Charité and her husband did not live happily ever after as we had supposed they would, for there was a villain. Here is another story that would be complete in itself without any reference to Charité's experience in the robbers' cave. The story begins with the rejected suitor who pretends to be a friend to the husband but treacherously kills him, and in such a way that no crime is suspected. Then follows the account of the murderer's unsuccessful attempts to win the affections of the widow; the appearance of the husband's spirit who comes to his wife in her sleep and tells her how his death was brought about; the terrible vengeance that Charité wreaked upon the murderer; the account of how she then killed herself at her husband's tomb, where she was buried and "left to be his bride for all eternity"; and last of all how the villain was overcome by remorse and had himself shut up in the same vault to starve to death. All this is told in great detail and with a vividness that could hardly be surpassed.

Lucius now enters on another phase of his life as an ass, and another long series of adventures follows. All readers of detective stories know that when the thrills come too thick and fast, they cease to be thrilling. So in this story the adventures of Lucius are so many and so varied that the variety itself becomes monotonous, and at this point the reader may want to stop to rest. The story of the ass goes on telling of his many vicissitudes, of how he was beset by one danger after another, danger from wolves, from mastiffs more terrible than wolves, and from villagers the most fierce of all. Once, when running away from a man who was trying to kill him, he broke into a house, upset the table in the dining-room where a banquet was going on, and then burst into a bedroom. There the people of the house thinking that the creature was mad locked him in, and the ass had a blissful night sleeping on a real bed again. He passed from one master to another until finally he came into the possession of two brothers, the cook and the baker of a rich man who was travelling in Thessaly. These slaves had a room in a lodging house, and as they had no other place to keep the ass, they took him into their own room. Here Lucius enjoyed life, for the slaves used to take home the delicious food that was left from their master's dinner-parties, and when they left the room, he had a glorious time feasting. He says that although he was an ass, he was not *such an ass* as to leave dainty viands and eat hay. When the brothers came home and found that the food which they had left in the room had disappeared they were much puzzled, and after it had happened again and again, each began to accuse the other of stealing it. After mutual recrimination they decided to pretend to go away as usual, but to watch through a crack in the door and see what did happen. When they saw the ass partaking of the viands with evident relish, they roared with laughter and called in one friend after another to see it. The laughter was so loud that the master of the slaves who happened to be passing the house stopped to see what it was all about, and he too was convulsed with amusement, and had the ass taken to his own dining-room and served with a regular dinner. He afterwards bought this remarkable animal from his slaves and appointed a freedman as his attendant. This man taught Lucius various tricks for the amusement of guests. He taught him to wrestle and to dance, to recline at the dinner-table, and even to answer questions by bowing his head for yes, and tossing it back for no, thus using that gesture of negation which is still common in Naples. The man into whose possession Lucius had now come was from Corinth and after a time he returned home taking the ass with him. The fame of Lucius had now spread far and wide and his owner began to charge an admission fee for seeing him.

The story is too prolonged to give in any detail, but the next part of special interest is the description of a pageant in which the judgment of Paris on Mount Ida was represented. The animated description with its great richness of detail indicates that the author is describing a spectacle which he had actually seen. After telling how Paris was bribed, Lucius remarks that he cannot wonder that there is corruption in the law-courts now, after such a precedent. He mentions two or three other legendary trials and then, with a fierce burst of indignation, he refers to the condemnation of Socrates. With that he starts on an appreciation of Socrates, but quickly checks himself, saying that people will not want to hear an ass talking philosophy.

With the coming of spring Lucius began to think more and more of the roses which would restore him to his own form, and when he learned of a disaster that threatened him, he determined to run away. There was no difficulty in doing this for he had long been so thoroughly domesticated that he was neither tied nor watched. He started off and ran as fast as he could for miles, until he came to the seashore where he sank down on the beach utterly exhausted and fell asleep. In the middle of the night he woke and found himself all alone there on the seashore. The full moon was just rising from the waves, more brilliant, more wonderful than he had ever seen it before, and all around him was the silent mystery of the night. The splendor of the moon, the beauty of the moonlight on the sea, the silence and the solemnity of it all aroused in him the thought of Deity, and he felt convinced that human life is not governed by chance, but that there is a Providence. More than ever before he was overwhelmed by the thought of his great calamity, and he prayed. He poured out his whole soul in prayer, prayer that was both worship and petition. He implored that he might be released from this foul semblance of a four-footed beast, that he might be restored to human form and become again his true self. With the prayer there came to him a wonderful sense of peace and trust, and again he slept. In his sleep he had a vision. A Deity appeared to him, the one "who rules the shining heights of heaven and the health-giving breezes of the sea," the Deity "who is worshipped throughout all the earth, though with varied rites and under many diverse names, the Deity to whom the Egyptians, mighty in ancient lore, have given the name of "Isis, Isis the Queen." The Deity assured Lucius that his prayer had been heard, that his petition would be granted. Then she told him that the next day was the time of the great Spring Festival which celebrated the opening of navigation. As one part of the ceremonies, she said, there would be a long procession, and in the procession he would see a priest with roses in his hand. The ass was to go up to the priest, stoop over as if to kiss his hand, and nibble the roses. The morning came and the festival began. The description of the pageant is very impressive, and so vivid that the reader seems to be seeing rather than reading. We see the ass as he stands on the side of the road in the midst of the crowd of spectators, we see one group after another in the long procession, and finally, a long distance away, the priest appears. Then as he draws nearer, Lucius, eagerly watching, sees the roses. He waits now in an agony of hope and fear, and it is all so clearly pictured that the reader's own heart begins to beat more quickly. The ass wonders how he can ever break through that great crowd of spectators to approach the priest. But just as the priest comes by, the people, of their own accord and not knowing why they do it, suddenly separate and open a path for the ass. The priest stops, knowing why he does it, for the Deity had appeared to him also in the night, and holds out the garland. Then all takes place just as had been promised — Lucius becomes a man again. And all the people who beheld it marvelled at the miracle, and the faithful bowed their heads.

The story goes on to tell how the priests and other friends furnished Lucius with all that he needed, and how in course of time he became a sincere and devout adherent of the Isis religion. This part of the story, telling as it does much of the various ceremonies and initiations, is of special interest for the light that it throws on the Isis worship which was such an important element in the Paganism of the later Empire.

After a time Lucius made a short visit to the home of his fathers in Africa, and then he set out for Rome. The thrill that he felt when he had really started for Rome was just what many others have felt all through the centuries from the first to the twentieth at the thought of being actually on the way to Rome.

This is a curious book, for although it began as fiction, it ends as autobiography. Somehow, and we cannot tell how or when, Lucius the Greek has become transformed into Lucius the African, and is to a certain extent identified with the author himself. The account of the religious experience is no fiction, but a glimpse into the genuine and the deepest experience of a human soul. In this there is a remarkable and beautiful prayer which would require only very slight changes to make it entirely suitable for a Christian church, for it is the devout expression of profound religious feeling. There are various indications that when the author began this story, he did not know himself how it was going to end, and the reader who follows it through can hardly fail to be convinced that the author had become a changed character. The man who prayed that prayer, who wrote the last book with its wonderful mysticism and its intense devotion, was a different man from the one who earlier in life had published a flippant and scurrilous defense in a scandalous trial, and who wrote together with beautiful and romantic stories, hideous tales of vice and crime.

The story as a whole is characterized by rollicking gaiety and the spirit of adventure. The style is extremely original, so original indeed that it is extraordinary. To a reader accustomed to the regularity, the restraint, and perfect self-control of classical Latin, the style of Apuleius is startling. One can easily believe that he learned Latin without a teacher, for his style of writing it is like nothing else in the language either before or since. Yet there is an indescribable fascination in it. It is complicated, intricate and often difficult, but rich, vivid, and picturesque. There is a certain magic quality in it which could not be reproduced in another language, and the story must inevitably pale in any attempt to tell it in English. Yet it is a story that whether read in one language or another the world will never entirely lose. Apuleius was not a great author nor a great man. But no one who reads much of his writings could fail to become interested in the man, and he produced a work which while not great is none the less immortal.

A SPANISH POET IN ROME

Of the many famous views in Rome (and of Rome) there is none perhaps better known than that from the Janiculum Hill, for that is one of the sights which even hurried tourists are urged to see. Standing on the Janiculum Hill at sunset we can see all Rome spread out before us, with the Campagna in its sunset colors beyond, and in the background are the distant hills with little towns and scattered villas nestling on the slope. This is one of the views that has been loved from earliest times, and no author has ever written of it with greater love and appreciation than a poet of the first century of our era.

No one who loves the view could fail to love this poem too, which describes the " seven sovereign hills " *septem dominos montes* of Rome, and, too, the Alban and the Tusculan hills. The poem refers to the cool retreats near the city, ancient Fidenae and little Rubrae, the Via Flaminia and the Via Salaria where the carriages may be seen, although no sound of wheels is heard. All these names are very familiar to those who know Rome to-day, and one can hardly read the poem without thinking of the poet who loved the Janiculum not only for its own sake but also because it was the home of one of his best friends.

He was an interesting character, this young Roman of Spanish birth, Marcus Valerius Martialis, who so loved the view from the Janiculum. Of his early life in Spain very little is known, but all that is known indicates that he had a happy boyhood in a refined though not wealthy home, and the many references to Spain in the poems show how deeply he loved the land of his birth. Bilbilis, his birthplace, was a Roman colony in Hispania Terraconensis, a province that had some of the finest schools of the Empire. It was situated on a rocky height above the river Salo, between the important towns of Emerita and Caesar Augusto (now called Merida and Saragossa). The scenery in this locality is wild and imposing, and must have made a deep impression on the poet in his boyhood. The town itself ceased to exist centuries ago, and even its name would be little known to-day if it were not for the references in Martial's poems. But his own love for his birthplace gives a remarkable vividness to all his allusions, and the reader cannot forget them.

At the age of twenty-three Martial left his home and went to Rome. He had doubtless already tried his hand at writing before this, although we know nothing of his earliest works. He had little money, but he had much ambition and he was full of eager hope. Nor was his hope without foundation, for he had very influential fellow-countrymen in Rome from whom he had reason to expect aid. Seneca, the statesman and philosopher, still had much power and great influence; Junius Gallio, brother of Seneca, it will be remembered, was proconsul of Achaea and presided at the trial of the Apostle Paul at Corinth; and the poet Lucan, nephew of Seneca, stood high in the favor of Nero at that time. Quintilian was in Rome too, both a lawyer of high reputation and one of the greatest teachers of all time. But unfortunately for Martial, very soon after his arrival in Rome a conspiracy against Nero's life was discovered which brought the whole Seneca family, unjustly perhaps, under suspicion, and their friendship was a disadvantage instead of an asset to a young author. As for Quintilian, the best advice that he could give him at this time was to give up writing, study law, and enter a profession for which Martial had as little ability as he had inclination. Quintilian generally gave good advice, but he was not infallible and the world may be glad that in this instance his advice was not followed. Another friend also urged Martial to become a lawyer, telling him that it was a lucrative profession. To him the poet replied that when a farm is profitable it is the farmer who makes it so, implying that the legal profession is profitable only for an able lawyer. He, fortunately for himself, recognized perfectly his own lack of ability in that line.

Just what Martial did do at first is not known, for there is no record of his first fifteen years in Rome. The silence itself is suggestive, for it indicates that these were years which he did not like to recall. It is probable that this was a period such as many another young author has experienced, a period of poverty and hardship with renewed disappointments and occasional days of black discouragement. It will be remembered that these years during which Martial was apparently unknown were very important years in Roman History. They included the horrible eighteen months that followed Nero's death and the accession of the Flavian Emperors when life in Rome again became normal.

Martial's first known publication was a little book of epigrams and short poems written to celebrate the opening of the Colosseum in the year 80 A.D. The chief interest in this work is the fact that it brought the author into public notice. The poems themselves are of little value, but although they were mere pot-boilers, they served their purpose. They did make Martial known to the reading public.

A few years after the *Liber Spectaculorum* [1] two other books were published, the *Xenia* and *Apophoreta*, a collection of couplets suitable to send with presents of various kinds. In many of these the sentiment is very gracefully expressed.

There are various references in the poems which show where Martial lived in Rome. First he lived in the third story of a house near the Portico of Agrippa on the Quirinal Hill. After the year 94 he had a small house of his own near the Temple of Quirinus. He also had a little country place at Nomentum, the modern La Mentana. There he spent many summers and went often at other times of year.

By the publication of the first book of epigrams Martial became not only well known in Rome, but very popular, and his popularity never waned. He was witty, genial, and warm-hearted, with unrivalled social qualities and a wonderful capacity for friendship. It is to be remembered, too, that the epigram itself was extremely popular at this time. Many writers attempted it and thousands of epigrams were written, but very few except those of Martial have survived.

This young poet from Spain saw all sides of life in Rome. He had the entrée to the best and most cultivated society as well as to circles less exclusive, and some of the most prominent men of the age were among his friends. He was a keen observer, and in his works we have kaleidoscopic pictures giving glimpses into a great city full of all sorts and conditions of people, representing every grade of society and every kind of life. It was a city

---

[1] These early works are misleadingly published at the end of the entire collection of epigrams.

with all the activities, all the interests, all the human joys and sorrows that any great modern city can have. Many of the epigrams are indeed concerned with the surface qualities of life, and some are seemingly insignificant. There are subjects which in the hands of any other poet would not have been worth touching, but Martial's vivid presentation gives them value. He has a wonderful power of presenting the trivial so exquisitely that one forgets that it is trivial.

The so-called epigrams of Martial are by no means all epigrams in the strict meaning of the term. There are letters, good wishes, birthday greetings, expressions of sympathy, epitaphs, glimpses of happy homes, and tributes to friends. The subjects on which he touches are so many and so varied that they defy any attempt at classification. Human life was his subject and his themes are a medley, as much a medley as is the average human life. There are many which might be called character sketches, and some of these characters are to be found in every age. We find the " migratory rich " of whom he says that those who live everywhere live nowhere. We meet the shopper who has all the contents of the shelves pulled down for him to look at, and finally buys something worth only a few pennies which had been on the counter all the time. Another is said to buy at a bargain, not because the price is low, but because he knows that he will never pay. There is a reference to the counters on the sidewalks which are still to be seen in Italy. In the time of Domitian this custom had become so common that it was a nuisance and Domitian issued a decree doing away with the abuse. In the epigram referred to, Martial expresses the gratitude of the city to Domitian saying that what was recently a track has now become a street; now it is Rome, where a little while ago it was a huge shop *Nunc Roma est, nuper magna taberna fuit.* There is the man who is so excessively polite that if he meets you ten times within an hour, he greets you each time as effusively as if he had not seen you for months. Martial's comment is that anyone who is so constantly saying to another, " How do *you* do? " can himself have nothing to do. Next comes one who is surly and disagreeable when all goes well with him, but becomes very affable if he is in trouble and needs help. Another was generous so long as he was poor, but when he inherited a fortune he became niggardly. There is the man who is always intending to do something great, but never does anything at all, because he cannot decide what his *magnum opus* shall be, and the one who gossips about other people's affairs when he might better be attending to his own. We meet a man going about as melancholy as if he had lost his last friend, not because of any grief or sorrow, but because he has not been invited out to dinner and so is forced to dine at home. Of another who boasts that he never does dine at home, Martial says that there is no exaggeration in his claim, for if he is not invited out, he does not dine at all. One enthusiastic dinner-guest comes so early that the host tells him he is too late for breakfast. There appears, too, a stingy host, who made a practice of inviting his friends to dinner when he knew that they had previous engagements. And we learn of a man who in his eagerness for birthday presents had at least eight birthdays a year. A bombastic lawyer is described, one who makes a long and would-be eloquent speech in which he alludes to all Roman history and " with his mighty voice and many a gesture he makes the court ring with Cannae and the Mithridatic War and insensate Punic Perjuries," and so on and on, when the case in which he is pleading is concerned only with the theft of three goats. There are various " grinds " on doctors too. In one of these a man who had been perfectly well in the evening is found dead in his bed the next morning. This sudden death is explained by the theory that the man must have dreamed of seeing a doctor.

There were plenty of bores in Roman society, as in all other society, and these we find in Martial. There is the gossip who " invents much and relates it as the truth "; the man who persists in talking although he has nothing to say, and the one who informs you that it is a warm day, as if he were imparting some important secret. One man annoyed Martial by asking him what sort of a person he would be if he should suddenly become rich and powerful. Martial replies, naturally enough, that he cannot tell, and then retorts, " If *you* should become a lion, what sort of lion would you be? " Worst of all bores perhaps was the poet who was so persistent in reciting his verses that all his friends fled whenever they saw him coming. To more than one man who asks why Martial does not send him his poems, the rather brusque reply is given, " Because I don't want you to send me yours." It must be remembered that literary activity was one of the features of the age. Writing was not merely the fashion, it was a fad. There were hordes of would-be authors, and authors' readings were so common that they are referred to as one of the trials of the day. In regard to certain poets among his contemporaries, Martial remarks that no one can be called an author whose works nobody reads; that that is not long from which there is nothing to be subtracted, but that some people are capable of making even distichs long. In another place he says, " If a man writes only distichs, his object, I suppose, is to please by brevity. But what is the use of brevity if there is a bookful of it?" Martial did not mean to be a bore himself, and in inviting a friend to dinner and giving a list of the attractions to be offered he adds, " I promise even more; I will recite nothing."

There are frequent complaints of plagiarism, but Martial resents more bitterly than having his own poems appear under another's name the fact that some people published under his name ill-natured epigrams that he never would have written. His own jests, while often sharp, were never ill-natured, and he refused to give the real names of the people whom he attacked. As he says in one epigram: " My page has not wounded even those whom it justly hates." This aroused curiosity and there were discussions at many a dinner-table as to whom he meant. Then would come another epigram, this one for instance, " I will not say, although you keep asking me, who is the Postumus in my little book. I will not say." Or this, " Do not ask me who this man is? I have forgotten." Martial says himself that his aim is " to spare the person but denounce the vice," and that he does not wish for fame won by another's blush. It may well be that in most of his invectives he did not have any actual individual in mind but was satirizing a vice, while the person to whom it was attributed was as imaginary as the name. Many people, however, amused themselves by trying to guess who was meant, while others who feared that the attack was on themselves had bitter feelings toward Martial.

Martial detested sham of all kinds and there are several epigrams on women who tried to appear younger than they were. There was Afra, for instance, who was always talking about her mammas and her papas, when she herself might be considered the great-grandmamma of all the papas and mammas. Another woman wears false hair and swears that it is her own, but it is no false oath that she takes, for she has bought the hair and paid for it. " That which you buy you can legally call your own," and Martial applies this also to the man who publishes as his own poems which he has bought from the author. The dandy was one of Martial's special aversions and also the " new rich," those whose ignorance was equal to the rapidly gained wealth of which they made vulgar display. One such man is said to have feigned illness because he wanted the doctor to see his beautiful bed blankets. The people who lived beyond their means are satirized also, and these seem to have formed a large class in Rome. The custom of kissing which was very prevalent Martial abhorred, and there are many references to it. One man who starts to kiss his friends in December is requested to put it off until April.

Many of the poems are in the form of letters and among them there is one to his old pedagogue, " the rocker of his cradle and the guardian of his boyhood," who never can realize that the boy of whom he had had charge has grown up. He still feels as responsible for the man as he had been for the child, and watches, and protests, and often says, " Your father never did that." This recalls Fronto's attitude in his old age toward Marcus Aurelius.

The age in which Martial lived was as notable for exaggeration as our own, and he often uses an exaggeration for emphasis, which it would be hard to duplicate anywhere except in America. His little place at Nomentum he might have said was small and insignificant. Instead he says that his garden is so small that it would not furnish a square meal to a single caterpillar, that there is not room for a mushroom to swell or violets to open, that the harvest when gathered hardly filled a snail-shell, and that all the wine was stored in a pitch-sealed nut-shell. One epigram describes very small mules by saying that the rider would be higher if he sat on the ground, and another tells of a stenographer whose speed was so remarkable that he could finish taking the dictation before the author had finished dictating. Referring to the lack of water at Ravenna, he says that an inn-keeper there cheated him because when he asked for wine and water, pure wine was brought, and that at Ravenna a cistern was more profitable than a vineyard. He also congratulates the owners of vineyards near Rome on the excessive amount of rain one season, because the water had thus become mixed with wine before the grapes were gathered.

The variety in the epigrams is so continuous that even the variety itself may sometimes become monotonous, but we must not omit the one which says that the wife should always be considered inferior to the husband, because in no other way can the equality of the sexes be maintained. And it is hard not to mention Issa, that dear little dog whose portrait had been painted, such a wonderful portrait that if you put the two together, the picture and the dog, " you will think that both are alive, or both are painted." Nor can one forbear to mention that other pet, Lydia, " savage in the woods and gentle at home," nor the man who cannot be included in Martial's poems because of his name which does not fit the meter. Nor can we forget the woman of Italian birth who tried to be effective by speaking Greek, nor yet the man who was angry at not being invited to an entertainment but not so angry as to be unwilling to annoy his host by attending.

The life of Rome in Martial's time was as strenuous, as full of varied interests and social distractions as that of any modern city to-day, and he often complains of the way in which he is forced to waste time. " Mightiest Rome wears us out." " Here when is a day my own? I am tossed on the deep ocean of the city, and my life is wasted in toil that brings no return." To a friend who has accused him of laziness because he has published only one book in a whole year, he replies that the wonder is that he has published even one, when the exacting social engagements take so much of his time that whole days slip away one after another with nothing accomplished. In another poem on the same subject he adds, " This is what happens when a poet is not willing to dine at home." But Martial enjoyed social occasions too much perhaps to be able to resist them, and he would not have been quite the same Martial if he could have resisted. It is evident however that as his fame increased he became more independent in taking time for writing and giving less and less to social obligations. For instance he says very frankly to a friend who lived on the other side of the Tiber, a long distance from the Quirinal where Martial lived, that he is glad to go to see him late in the day, but that he cannot spoil a whole morning by going to the morning reception. To the host at a large reception, he says, one guest more or less makes little difference, but it makes a great difference to himself if he loses a whole morning. In another poem which he sends to a friend with a book just finished, he says, " If Proculus asks why I did not go myself, tell him that these poems such as they are could not have been written by anyone who spends his time going to receptions."

The noise of the city Martial found very wearing and he frequently refers to it. There is no place in the city, he says, for either thinking or resting, for " all Rome was at his bedroom door." Some people would say that in this respect Rome has not changed much since Martial's day.

There are many complaints of poverty in the poems, but these should not be taken too seriously. Martial was certainly far from rich, not so much because he did not have money as because he could not keep it. He apparently had a habit of letting his expenses exceed his income, but it should be said in his defence that Rome was an exceedingly expensive city where people more prudent than he found difficulty in making ends meet.

Two or three poems sarcastically inquire what use there is in an education when people who lack it can become rich, and the fame of a poet is no greater than that of a race-horse. " Don't devote yourself to the Muses," he says. " None of those girls will give you cash." But while he does sometimes complain of poverty and lament that so little money can be made by writing, yet in a serious mood he says, " Even if my poems bring me no profit, they are my own delight." And they have been the delight of many readers all through the ages. One revels still in the beauty of the Roman spring, just as beautiful to-day as in the poet's time when he wrote, " Wherever you turn your eyes or wandering steps you see every path ruddy with twining roses." One treads with joy again with him " the ridges Bacchus loved " on old Vesuvius, " the haunt of Venus " now " drowned in fire and melancholy." One wanders with the book he sent from his home on the Quirinal to his friend Proclus on the Palatine and rejoices in the references he made to various buildings whose ruins are still standing, the Temple of Castor near that of Vesta, the house of the Vestals, and the Sacra Via where he says there were many portraits (statues) of Domitian and Cybele's dome.

There is much in Martial's work that this essay does not touch upon, for it would prolong the essay beyond reasonable limits to attempt anything like a complete presentation. It is inevitable perhaps when an author writes as much as Martial did, that much of his work will be inferior to the best. We must go farther than that in his case and say that some of his poems are dull, that the point, even when well made, was not worth making, and that some of his writings are worse than dull. That fact however does not detract from the value of the best, and in justice to Martial it should be noted that in comparison with the whole number of his poems the proportion of those which ought never to have been written has been grossly exaggerated by critics of a certain class. The entire number of the objectionable epigrams at the outside estimate is not more than one-seventh of the whole, and yet one who had never read Martial but read what some of his critics have said of him would think that his themes were all objectionable and would get a totally wrong impression of the man. His own judgment of his work is well known, that it includes the good, the indifferent, and the bad, and to enjoy Martial one should be able to ignore the bad, neglect the indifferent, and read the good.

Martial himself would have been both surprised and amused if he had imagined that he would ever be considered an " instructive writer," but his works furnish such a mine of information on so many topics connected with Roman life that they must be listed among the sources for that study, and so the term is not so inappropriate as he would have thought it.

Many people have thought of Martial as being merely a wit, but he was much more than that, and more than once he tells the reader that these little poems are not all jokes, that there are serious ones also, and it may be added that some of those in a more serious vein are among the best. Three of Martial's most attractive qualities are his love of the country, his love of little children, and his devotion to his friends. While Martial was essentially a man of the town who with keen sight and shrewd appraisal observed and set forth, often in very few but telling words, the fashions and the follies, the vices and the virtues, the lights and the shades of city life, there was nothing that he loved better than the beauties of nature. A description of his friend's villa on the Janiculum with its gardens " more blessed than the gardens of the *Hesperides*" finds its way into his poetry. Another poem describes the villa of a friend at Formiae on the Mediterranean coast, that delightful retreat on the shore where " the sea's surface quivers in the wind, and bears the painted boat before the breeze," a breeze so gentle that it is compared to that caused by " the fluttering of a girl's purple fan." After describing the charms of the spot, Martial speaks of how often the owner of a great country estate can enjoy it himself for short periods only, for he is held in the city by its pressing affairs. The master owns the villa, but it is the servants, he says, who spend all their time there to whom it really belongs. Various poems refer to other villas in places well known still as resorts, Anxur near the sea, and Tibur. One gives a detailed description of the villa of a friend at Baiae. This was really a farm where no space was left untilled and Martial describes the work of various kinds which goes on. He refers also to the social pleasures, calls from other country people many of whom bring gifts from their own farms. " When work is done a cheerful neighbor is invited to dinner." The whole picture is of peaceful busy lives, where the work is hard but worth doing, and the unbought pleasures as enjoyable as they are simple.

There is a poem, written just before Martial left Rome to return to Spain, about his own little estate at Nomentum. This is in the form of a letter to a friend whom he asks to care for the estate after he goes away and especially to keep up the sacred rites. He speaks of the twin pines, the ornaments of an untrimmed grove, of the holm-oaks, and of the rude altars to various deities, made by his overseer's unskilled hand. The whole tone of the poem shows how Martial loved this little farm which had long been his retreat when he wanted a rest from the noise and confusion of Rome. It closes by asking his friend whenever he offered sacrifice to " these gentle deities of a little field " to include this in his prayer — " Wherever your Martial is, he too with me is offering sacrifice to you, an absent priest. Consider that he is here and grant to both of us whatever either shall pray for."

The poems above referred to all have reference to the beauties of a cultivated villa, but Martial had great love also for the wild mountainous scenery near his early home in Spain and in his latest years in Rome he was constantly thinking of that.

Martial's love of children is expressed in various poems and among his most charming epigrams are those about a little slave girl Erotion of whom he was very fond. This child died when she was not quite six years old, but she will always be remembered by anyone who reads Martial. The first of these poems about the little Erotion is addressed to his own father and mother who had died many years before. He asked them to receive the little one when she went alone into the next world and take care of her so that she might not be afraid, this little girl who had been, as he says " his sweetheart and his darling, his playfellow and his joy."

Two other poems refer to a portrait of a young friend of Martial made when he was a child. These are especially interesting because so many and such charming portrait busts of children still exist. Then there was another child friend of Martial whose name one knows, Glaucias, a beautiful boy who had just begun his thirteenth year when he died, " a brief-lived darling for whom all Rome grieves." And even a baby's rattle is made the subject of a couplet.

Capacity for friendship is perhaps the most outstanding of Martial's characteristics, and few writers have ever given it more charming expression. The list of his friends would be a long one and there is no greater tribute to his personality than we see in the kind of people who loved him. They may not all have admired his genius any more than did the younger Pliny, whose tone, while very affectionate, was a little patronizing, but they all appreciated his personal qualities. Some of the poems written to individual friends are among the finest of all that he wrote. There is a letter to one of his oldest friends on his sixtieth birthday, Julius Martialis, who had the beautiful villa on the Janiculum. In another letter Martial gives a little retrospect of their intimacy which had continued for thirty-four years. During these years the sweets and the bitters had been mingled, as in most human lives, but the pleasant things outnumbered the others. " If all the pebbles should be sorted, the white ones on one side and the dark on the other, the white heap would be larger." Another poem is dedicated to the library of Julius Martialis, and this was sent with a copy of his first seven books, hoping that his own works would have a place in that library, as they undoubtedly did.

Among the letters there are several written as birthday greetings, and in one of these he implies that the most appropriate gift that a poet can send is a poem. There are two epigrams on the birthday of a neighbor at Nomentum, Quintus Ovidius, who was born on the first of April, and Martial, as we remember, on the first of March. In this poem he says the calends of March gave him life, but the calends of April gave him a friend, and that was the greater gift.

There are interesting allusions to some of the fine Roman women whom Martial knew. One is a tribute to a woman of British ancestry but who had the feelings of the Latin race — " Italian mothers think she is Roman, while those of Attica claim her as their own." Other epigrams are addressed to Polla, the widow of the poet Lucan for whom Martial had great admiration and whom he considered second only to Virgil as a poet. There is an interesting poem about Sulpicia, a poet of the time. She and her husband were among Martial's good friends, and Martial seems to have had great admiration for Sulpicia's poetry, although none of it has survived. Speaking of a friend's portrait which he " honors with violets and roses," he says, " Would that art could portray his character and mind; more beautiful in all the world would no painting be." There are charming poems on happy marriages and glimpses into some of the delightful homes where Martial often went and where he was always a welcome guest. Nor was it his personal friends only whom Martial appreciated. Sham and pretence he loathed but for genuine goodness he had profound respect. In the letters to his friends there is little of the caustic wit which characterizes many of his other poems, but always a delightful geniality. One feels in them the absolute sincerity of the man, his warm heart and his love of good fellowship. It is in these letters too that Martial's serious thought is most frequently expressed. Friendship is not to be gained by words. " It is by loving that one comes to be loved." He moralizes, for instance, very much in the vein of Seneca or of a modern preacher on true freedom as something which a man can give himself. " The man who does not like anyone is a man to be pitied." "It makes a great difference whether you are really good or wish to seem so." Sayings such as these are numerous. In his tribute to Quintilian, Martial justifies his own desire to enjoy life, and in more than one poem he urges that *living* should not be put off till to-morrow. "He is wise who lived yesterday," for the future is uncertain, but the past is our own. "He lives twice who can enjoy the life that has gone by." One of the best poems is that which gives the essentials of a happy life: "Means not acquired by labor but bequeathed; fields not unkindly, an ever-blazing hearth, no lawsuit, the toga seldom worn, a quiet mind, a healthy body, congenial friends, good-natured guests, a board plainly spread . . . sleep such as makes the darkness brief; be content with what you are . . . nor dread your last day, nor long for it."

Martial lived in Rome for nearly thirty-five years continuously except for a stay in Gallia Cisalpina where his third book was written. This was sent to Rome from Cornelii Forum, now called Imola. He implies in the preface that this book could not be expected to be as good as those written in Rome — "The home-born book ought to surpass the Gaul." He became familiar also with other towns, for he refers to the charms of Altinum, a town near Venice, and Aquileia, as being pleasant places for a retreat in old age.[2] Martial was especially pleased by his popularity in Vienna, the modern Vienne, and it now gives pleasure to the modern reader of Martial who visits Vienne to find that they still have a street named for him.

It is significant that Martial, although he lived in Rome so many years, although he had so many good friends in Rome, in his later years felt an increasing desire to go back to the friends of his boyhood, to return home to his native Spain. His love for Spain and his pride in Spain are shown by many allusions in his poems. That localized patriotism which was so characteristic of the Romans of the Empire, Martial had in a high degree, and that corner of the world, that *angulus terrarum,* as Horace says,

[2] The reference to the latter town is of interest because of recent excavations there and a fine archaeological museum, which is especially rich in tomb inscriptions of great variety, including some types not found elsewhere. These excavations were begun in 1929 and they are yielding interesting results. There are some fine examples of mosaic pavements that Martial may have seen, for some of them are not later than the early Augustan period.

grew more and more dear to him as he grew older, but his love for Spain is in evidence all through his works. We know how proper names, names of places, if they combine beauty of sound with interest of association are often very effective in poetry, but Martial so loved the association that uncouthness of sound did not trouble him and he took real pleasure in introducing some of the rough Spanish names in his poems, " Peteius blushing with its roses, the shallows of little Tuetonissa, Buradon's sacred oak-wood, and the pleasant grove of Boterdus." Peteius and Tueto-nissa, Buradon and Boterdus and various others to which Martial refers cannot be called melodious names, but Martial loved them none the less.

Martial never lost his pride in his home town nor his affection for his old neighbors and family friends, and among the poems there are a number of letters to friends in Spain. Martial had always meant to return to Spain some day but he was never able to go for a visit, as Catullus often went to Verona and Pliny to Como. The journey was long and expensive, and Martial's in-clination to spend money when he had it constantly prevented his saving enough for a trip to Spain. Had he been able to do this he might have changed his mind about wanting to return to Bilbilis to live. As it was, he resolved more and more firmly as the years went on that he would return at some time, that Bilbilis should be his home, the home of his old age as it had been of his boyhood. He had become tired in Rome. It is in his latest epi-grams for the most part that we find the complaints of the noise of Rome and of his suffering from being unable to sleep. Rome was a very expensive city to live in, too, quite as expensive as either Rome or any American city to-day, and Martial longed for a place where he could have greater comfort at less cost, where " small means make one rich," where he could be " the tiller of a field that was not large but was his own." Finally the time came when he could really make definite plans for going, and among the latest of the poems written in Rome there is a letter to his fellow-townsmen in Bilbilis to tell them that he is coming. They must be prepared to see some changes in him — " For four and thirty years I have dwelt within the stately walls of Madame Rome and the Italian realm has changed the color of my hair." Surely no reader would be so unkind as to suggest that when a man is nearly sixty years old a change in the color of the hair may not be entirely due to climate. The last poem in the tenth book is addressed to the book itself which he is sending to a friend in Spain, and he describes the journey which the book will take. He does not say from what port it will sail, but it will go " across the wide sea to Spanish Tarragona, and thence by carriage to Bilbilis, arriving there on the fifth stage." On this journey if Martial were taking it himself, he might see various friends and acquaintances, and so he tells the book to greet any comrades whom it sees. They were few now, these friends, but they were old ones, and it was thirty-four years ago that Martial last saw them. Then he asks Flavus, the friend to whom the book is sent, to find for him " at a healthy price " some " retreat," pleasant but not hard to keep up, a retreat where he can be lazy.

Martial would probably not have wanted a large estate even if he could have afforded it. What Flavus found for him we do not know, but we do know that a rich woman who was one of his Spanish friends made him a present of a small estate after his return to Spain. All the references to Marcella show not only gratitude but great admiration for her ability and her character. Although Spanish by birth she was worthy to be a Roman bride.

One of his friends in Rome had expressed surprise that Martial talked so much about far-off nations and that he should want to return to the Tagus and the Solo after he had grown old in Latium's city, and Martial explains that the simplicity of life in Spain is what he longs for now. That land is dear to him where small means make one rich, and the country house with its simple abundance seems in prospect very attractive.

It is well known that very few of the authors famous in Roman literature were born in Rome. But they lived in Rome, they were Romans of the city. Many of them, indeed, retained affectionate memories of their birthplaces, and went back from time to time; but to the others it was Rome and not the place where they had lived as children, that was home. Martial, although he was a loyal citizen of the Empire, never became really a Roman of the City. During his thirty-four years of residence, and constant mingling in Roman society he continued to be not a Roman but a Spanish poet in Rome.

It is noticeable that he who has been called, and with good

reason so called, " the most pronounced cosmopolitan poet in all antiquity " was the very one who chose to leave the great capital, the cosmopolitan city abounding in interests of many kinds, and return to the insignificant town in a far away province where he was born. In returning to Spain, therefore, he was carrying out a resolve which had been made probably early in his stay in Rome. That he should have idealized his early home to some extent during the long years that he was away from it was natural, and that some disappointments awaited him when he returned to it was inevitable. No one returning to his early home after a continuous absence of more than thirty years could find it just as he remembered it, and Martial was no exception. He enjoyed it all at first. There was a certain thrill in being again among the old familiar scenes. It was a joy to see again the old friends, the friends of his boyhood. But after a time the novelty wore off, the quiet became monotonous, the simple life to which he had so long looked forward began to pall, and more and more his thoughts turned back to Rome. Many of the old friends and neighbors in Bilbilis had passed away, and those who were left, although they gave him affection, could not give him the intellectual companionship that he craved. He himself remarked in one of his poems that a new friend may sometimes become an old comrade. That is very true, and it is equally true that an old friend cannot in all cases be a real comrade. There was really very little in common between Martial and those old friends of his in Bilbilis. The reminiscences of boyhood, the references to his parents from the old people who had known them, and all other subjects of mutual interest were soon exhausted, and Martial found that references to his life in Rome aroused envy and jealousy instead of interest. He suffered, too, from the petty criticisms and the gossip which are so often rife in a small place where, as he says, " one or two disagreeable people are a host." He missed keenly the libraries and theatres and social gatherings of Rome where he had sought and found the themes for many of his epigrams, but where he enjoyed it all so much that he hardly realized that he was working too. In Bilbilis he began to realize how much of his inspiration had come from his readers and from the companionship of those who understood as well as loved him, and he soon found himself longing for many things that he had been glad to leave when he went away from Rome. In Rome he had often complained of the interruptions, the distractions, the frittering away of his time, leaving so little for his writing. In Spain his days were all his own. He had few interruptions, no receptions to attend, plenty of time to write, and yet he could not write. He feared moreover that anything that he might write in Spain would have a Spanish flavor and lack the sparkle of his earlier works. Thus the earlier part of his stay in Spain after the first excitement was over was rendered melancholy by crushing homesickness, by that Romesickness which many people know is the worst kind of homesickness, and for three years he wrote little and sent nothing to Rome.

It is good to know, however, that, although during his first years in Spain he wished many times that he had never left Rome, his regret was not permanent, though he did feel occasional unutterable longing for Rome and Roman friends. Martial was at heart a provincial and the time came when he could write to his friend Juvenal that it was in Bilbilis he chose to live, and it was there that he wished to die.

Although for three years Martial felt no inclination to write, his friends were eager for another book, and when Priscus, who was also a Spaniard, returned to Spain, Martial sent him a little book of epigrams to greet him on his arrival. This, however, was not written with the same zest as his earlier works,[3] for he says, " I have ordered myself to do as a task what I used to indulge in as a pleasure."

Martial was himself in doubt as to whether this book should be sent to Rome or not, and leaves it to Priscus to decide. Priscus apparently did send it to Rome at once, and we can imagine that many of Martial's Roman friends read it through, as he himself says, " with eyes not over dry," and hoped that the next book would come soon. But the next book never came, for it was not very long after this that Martial died.

Although this last book was written in Spain, there are not many poems in it which refer especially to Spain, but one describes the small estate which Marcella had given him. It is a

---

[3] This was the twelfth and last book of Martial's epigrams, or rather a part of it, for Book XII, as we have it, is probably an enlarged edition of the book sent to Priscus and includes some epigrams that had been written earlier.

" little kingdom," he says, but he prefers it to the gardens of Alcineus which were proverbial for their beauty and luxury.

The social and antiquarian value of Martial's work has never been lost sight of, but its literary value is no less. He had not only great power as a satirist, he had true poetic ability also. In vigor and terseness of expression he has had few equals in any language. His style is difficult to describe and impossible to reproduce in another language. In most translations whether in verse or prose even if the point is not blunted as it so often is, yet the poise, the simplicity, the lightness of touch, the delicacy and the exquisite finish are lost.

The age in which Martial lived was characterized by startling contrasts, and he was as much a mass of contradictions as the age itself. He was both sharp and tender, caustic and kind, critical and tolerant, sarcastic and genial. He was frivolous, and yet serious, an uncompromising realist, brutally realistic at times, but not lacking ideals. His was not a strong character, but he was sincere, genuine, and unaffected. He was capable of fine feeling and he had a very lovable nature. It took courage to stay in Rome after Seneca's downfall had left him without influential friends, courage, and confidence in himself to keep on for so many hard years. Courage made him see the amusing side of life in general, and the amusing side of his own misfortunes. When he could write of his own poverty in such a way as to make his readers smile, we may be sure that he smiled himself while he was writing. Most of Martial's critics have taken him too seriously, and treated his jokes, which were no more meant to be understood literally than the squibs in " Punch," as if they were sober statement of solemn fact.

The secret of Martial's success lay in the knowledge of his own powers. He had the rare good judgment to keep to that which he knew he could do well, in spite of the exhortations of his friends to try something greater, and the sneers of his critics because he wrote trifles only.

The themes of Martial's works as a whole could not be better described than he himself describes them in four words, *hominem pagina nostra sapit*. It is that of which Life can say *meum est*.

Some of Martial's contemporaries may have been surprised at the absolute confidence with which he predicted the immortality of his own works.   Many people may have thought, as Pliny did, that such light poems could not be expected to live through the ages, but Martial himself was sure that they would, and he had no hesitation in saying:

> " This song of mine which cannot be destroyed
> by any chance or by the ' lapse of years '
> shall live when the works of Apelles shall
> perish."

The town where Martial was born and where he died ceased to exist centuries ago, and his own ashes have long been mingled with the dust of the native land that he loved so well, but a prophecy which he once made is still being fulfilled, that long after the mighty tombs on the Appian Way should be nothing but shapeless ruins, these little poems would still be read, and read in foreign lands.

CHARITIES AND PHILANTHROPIES IN THE ROMAN EMPIRE

> " Anyone who will spend a few days, or even a few well-directed hours, in examining the inscriptions of the Roman Empire, will find many a common, self-complacent prejudice melting away."

(Dill, in *Roman Society from Nero to Marcus Aurelius.*)

THE truth of the statement above is soon realized by anyone who gives even a little real study to that great period in human history which has been aptly described as a period " calumniated rather than known." For intelligent study of the life of the Roman Empire, it is necessary to put aside many prevalent notions, to try to forget pre-conceived ideas, and approach the subject with minds unbiased. False opinions are generally held with great tenacity, and there is nothing more difficult to change than conceptions based on ignorance. Much of the censure of the time, so common in the works of moralists of the past, is to be ascribed to the lack of knowledge. Dill remarks in another passage that the indictment of the Roman Empire " had degenerated into ignorant commonplace, when modern scholarship began to correct the exaggerations," and, unfortunately, commonplace ignorance of the time is much more widely spread than are the results of modern scholarship. Many people know of the evil who know nothing of the good. People are familiar with the iniquities of Nero, for instance, who have little knowledge of the " Five Good Emperors " whose successive reigns covered nearly a century, or of such men and women as Musonius, and Thrasea, and Helvia, and Paulina, and countless others of Nero's contemporaries. " Nero fiddled while Rome was burning." That is so indelibly impressed on the imagination of posterity that the words are glibly repeated to this day by people whose knowledge of the history of the Western world between the years 54 and 68 of our era is practically confined to those six words. But this statement, be it true or false, is of little importance in studying the history of

Nero's principate, or in learning of Roman society in general in
the time of the Empire. In the first century as well as later,
while there was indeed much of evil, there was also a movement
toward higher standards of life, and a demand for moral teaching.
In the works of Seneca, for instance, we may find frequent expression of this consciousness of spiritual need, frequent reference
to the multitudes who were, as he says, " stretching out their
hands for help." There were many preachers, and in some of
their utterances which have survived, moralists of to-day may
find inspiration as well as satisfaction. Nor did these preachers
stand alone. They were as much a product of their time as any
of the vicious who have become better known to posterity.
Juvenal's scathing satires were not written for those whose vices
he attacked, but for the larger number whose condemnation of
vice was no less than his own. Even the pessimistic Tacitus
pays a tribute to those who showed that " there can be good men
even under bad Emperors," and Martial refers with admiration to
the men and women " who in evil times had the courage to be
good." In the attempted comparisons between the Roman period
and modern times it has been the fashion to compare the good
of the present with the evil of the past, and thus exhibit the contrast between vice and virtue. But for a just view, we must compare the good of the present with the good of the past, or the
evil of the past with the evil of the present, and when we do that
no such startling contrast appears. Anyone who tries to compare
the time of the Roman Empire with our own time should remember that the evils of the Roman Empire were just as distressing
to the good men and women of that time as the evils of the present
are to the good men and women of to-day. In any single period
human society presents startling contrasts. At any time both
optimists and pessimists may always find abundant evidence to
support their views. One might make a study of almost any
century in history and by presenting only the evil make it seem
worse than any other century, or by presenting only the good
make it appear the best of all. It was true of the Roman Empire, as of every other period in the world's history, that good and
evil existed side by side. Then, as now and as always, there were

> " men that were good,
> and men that were bad,
> and men that were such as I."

And in trying to become acquainted with the life of the Roman Empire, it is the " men that were such as I " who are in some respects of the greatest interest. To understand Rome's success, we must look behind the leaders, beyond the few great men who stand far above their contemporaries, to the ordinary men and women, for it was they who were the real Roman people. They were the ones who kept the best of Roman traditions alive and handed them on to generation after generation. And for learning of those whose names were unknown to history, it is to the inscriptions, to the abiding records in stone, that we must turn. The memorials of obscure lives that we find here are indeed extremely brief, but brief though they are, they are extremely valuable for anyone who is interested in the people of the Roman Empire. There is a peculiar fascination in the Latin inscriptions because they transport one so completely into the time when they were written. Between ourselves and the Latin authors whose works we read in books, there is a long succession of copyists and editors, but when we stand before a piece of marble and read the words cut into its surface, there is no copyist there to come between the author and the reader. Through literature we may come very close to the minds of some of the greater men of the past. Through inscriptions we may get glimpses into the lives of some of the obscure, and for the study of Roman society, both kinds of evidence should be used. So much of human life is commonplace that we need the commonplace remains as well as the greater for gaining a true conception of life in the Roman Empire. Much study of this period, it may be said, makes one inclined to doubt the assertion of the poet, and declare instead, *Tempora mutantur, sed nos* NON *mutamur in illis.*

It used to be taken for granted that charity and philanthropy were virtues, not only characteristic of Christianity, but peculiar to Christianity and quite unknown in the Pagan world. That assumption however is one of the many errors which modern scholarship has been correcting. Even a little study of the evidence will show that not only was the public spirit which manifested itself in lavish gifts to the community at large a characteristic of the age, but that help for the needy, compassion for the wretched, and sympathy for the unfortunate were not exceptional, but common. It is to be remembered in the first place that one of the features of life in this period was the co-operation of the state and the individual citizen in providing those things which were either needed or desired by the public. Government aid and private generosity united for serving the interests of the community as a whole, and individual needs were not neglected. For the relief of poverty, something that every community must consider, systematic measures were often taken by the government, and one of the best of these was the special effort which was made in times of scarcity to keep the prices of provisions down. In the reign of Tiberius, for instance, when the people were uttering loud complaints about the cost of living, complaints that seem very modern, the Emperor limited the price of grain which a seller might demand. But for every measure sold, he himself paid the dealer a certain sum in addition. Since Tiberius was not a man to squander money or to give without reason, it is evident that in this way he made it possible for the people to buy grain at a price for which no dealer could afford to sell it. Antoninus Pius in a time of scarcity bought wheat, wine, and oil at his own expense and distributed them to the people free of charge. He also loaned money at the lowest rate ever exacted, " that he might use his fortune to aid as many people as possible." Similar measures were taken by other Emperors in Rome, by magistrates in the provinces, and by the local government in towns. That towns sometimes had a special fund for the assistance of the poor, is shown by a passage in the Digest.

Instances of aid given to individuals are not as likely to be recorded as benefactions which affected whole groups or classes of people, but there is evidence of the former kind of benevolence also. The Emperor Tiberius, for instance, assisted the deserving poor, as we learn from a passage in Tacitus. Among the many good deeds of Trajan that of helping individuals who needed help was not the least. Hadrian contributed to the support of certain poor women, and Alexander Severus was always helping the poor.

Not only were measures such as have been described taken by the government, but individuals also often gave help to the poor in the towns where they lived. The younger Pliny's kindness and generosity in private as well as public benefactions are well known, and that Pliny was no exception, there are a multitude of inscriptions to bear witness. Of one man it is said that he often came to the assistance of the people in hard times. Another sold grain at a very low price in times of scarcity, and of many others it is recorded that they used their own money to give help to the needy. On the tombstone of an old man in Sardinia we find the statement that he was the Father of Orphans, the Refuge of the Needy, the Protector of Strangers. A pearl merchant in Rome is said to have been " good, compassionate, and one who loved the poor." And to an old woman in Africa who died at the age of eighty-one years, a beautiful tribute was paid in the few words which state that she had been " a mother to everybody and a universal helper." The added testimony that in her long life she had " never made anyone unhappy " would be rare in any age. The instances which have been cited are only a few of the many which might be collected.

In many respects the city life of the Roman Empire, and especially that of the Antonine Age, was very similar to the city life of our own day. This problem of the poor, and especially in great cities, is one which confronts every age and which has never been completely solved, but attempts to meet the need were certainly not lacking in the Roman Empire.

Another excellent measure, and not uncommon, was the providing of free medical attendance for those who were not able to pay for such services. There are instances of individual physicians who gave their services free of charge to the poor, and as early as the time of Strabo certain towns, Marseilles for one, had employed physicians at public expense. But the regular organization of public medical attendance dates from the reign of Antoninus Pius. At that time the number of physicians in any town who were paid by the government was fixed in proportion to the population. The salaries in each town were determined by the municipal councillors, and the chief duties of such physicians were in the attendance on the poor, although they were not debarred from private practice also. There are many inscriptions which refer to public physicians and indicate the respect in which they were held. Money was sometimes given by private citizens also to provide free medicine for those who could not afford to pay for it. Several inscriptions might be quoted which refer to such funds. In this connection it is interesting to notice Dr. Singer's statement that " the great contribution of Rome to medicine is the hospital system." [1]   Hospitals, which are mentioned by authors of the first century, were at first private institutions, but some of these developed into public hospitals supported either wholly or in part by the government. The sites of several military hospitals, according to Singer, have been found, and of one of these, that at Novaesum near Düsseldorf, it has been possible to ascertain the plan somewhat in detail. This hospital was founded about the beginning of the second century, and Singer says of it, " The general scheme is much in advance of any military hospital until quite modern times." That the military *valetudinaria* should be followed soon by other public hospitals was natural.

The public banquets which were a characteristic and important feature of town life should be mentioned. Such banquets were often given by the wealthy citizens, and as all the people of the town were invited, regardless of class distinction or social position, they gave a good meal in many cases to people who sometimes went hungry. These public dinners were useful also to some extent in helping to bring about that acquaintance between different classes in society, between the rich and the poor, which many of the " social service " or " welfare " workers of our own day are trying to effect.

The maintenance of destitute children is something which every town must consider, and this seems to have been a common form of benevolence in the Roman Empire. Nerva was perhaps the first Emperor to make provision for the children of needy parents throughout Italy, but to Trajan belongs the honor of instituting a great endowment for this purpose. This is of special interest as being the prototype of similar institutions in our own time. The Emperor's desire was, as the younger Pliny says, that these children should be cared for by the state in such a way that their children would not need the aid of the state. This endowment of Trajan was a magnificent benefaction and merits the great enthusiasm with which Trajan's contemporaries received it. Two original documents, large bronze tablets, referring to this benefaction of Trajan are still in existence. One which was found not far from Benevento is now in the National Museum in Rome, and

[1] See Legacy of Rome, p. 293 ff., article by Charles Singer, Lecturer in the University of London.

the other, found at Velleia, is in the Parma Museum. The latter *tabula alimentaria,* as it is called, had been broken up and used as old metal, but the pieces were finally collected from the various places to which they had been scattered and with great difficulty fitted together again. The tablet measures six by ten feet, and the inscription is one of the longest ever found. Coins were struck in memory of the event, and in one of those marble balustrades in the Forum with which everyone acquainted with the Forum is familiar, this benefaction of Trajan is commemorated by a group of statuary. It is commemorated also in a similar way on the Arch of Trajan at Benevento. We may notice that this endowment of Trajan, while its primary object was the support of poor children, furnished assistance also to many small farmers by lending them money for an indefinite period at a low rate of interest.

The Emperors who succeeded Trajan established similar endowments. Antoninus Pius gave such a fund in memory of his wife Faustina, and the girls who had the benefit of it were called Faustinianae in her honor. Marcus Aurelius commemorated his wife in the same way, and in the next century Alexander Severus established such an endowment in honor of his mother.

Private citizens as well as Emperors gave money for the support of destitute children. The younger Pliny, among his numerous benefactions to his native town, established a fund for this purpose. A woman in the province of Tarragona in Spain left a legacy for the support of a hundred boys and girls. Another Spanish woman and a woman in Terracina gave similar funds, and a man in Africa entrusted to his " dearest fellow-townsmen " a sum of money for the support of three hundred boys and two hundred girls every year. Many more such instances might be added. It is interesting to notice in some of the tomb inscriptions of children that the fact that the child had had the benefit of such a foundation is sometimes recorded as a sort of distinction.

One of the characteristics of the present age is the liberality with which the whole civilized world comes to the aid of any community which has suffered a great public calamity. That this is true of our own age we may well rejoice, but it is also gratifying to learn that such expression of human sympathy is not confined to modern humanity. Both in literature and in inscriptions we find record of disasters similar to those of recent times and similar attempts to help the sufferers. Earthquakes were a frequent source of disaster in various parts of the Empire, and there are many instances of aid given to sufferers from this cause. In the time of Tiberius, for instance, there was a violent earthquake in Asia which caused the destruction of twelve cities. For the aid of these, a large sum of money was immediately sent by the Emperor, all taxes were remitted for a term of years, and a commissioner was sent from the senate to ascertain what was especially needed and take measures to procure it.

Another disaster which occurred in the reign of Tiberius was the collapse of the amphitheatre at Fidenae, a town a few miles from Rome. This came during the games when there were thousands of people in the building, and the number of killed and injured was very large. Immediately the wealthy families of Rome opened their homes to receive those who had been injured, medical aid was furnished, and every possible effort made to alleviate suffering.

Soon after this disaster at Fidenae there was a serious fire in Rome, and again both the Emperor and private citizens came to the help of those who suffered. On this occasion Tiberius gave liberal aid to individuals, not waiting to be asked, Tacitus says, but of his own accord seeking out people who needed help.

At a later period help was sent to the city of Bologna, which had suffered from fire, and to Lyons also. The city of Lyons had previously come to the aid of Rome after the great fire in the time of Nero. Instances of aid sent to people far away should be especially remembered, because munificent gifts to the home town were so common that the other kind of liberality has not been so much noticed.

Instances of help to sufferers similar to those which have been cited might be multiplied, but one more must suffice, the measures taken by Nero after the great fire in Rome. The popular indignation which was aroused against Nero by the report that he had enjoyed the spectacle of the fire has never died away, and has served to increase the deserved infamy that rests on Nero's name. That a great fire is a magnificent spectacle no one can deny, and that Nero may have imprudently shown his admiration of the wonderful sight is entirely possible. " Nero fiddling while Rome was burning," will never be forgotten, while a fact not so well known, although of far greater importance as far as the people were concerned, is that the measures taken by Nero for the relief of sufferers were both wise and energetic. From Tacitus, who gives a list of these measures, we learn that Nero opened his own gardens to the destitute and had various public buildings made available in the same way; that temporary shelters were very quickly erected; that arrangements were made for having provisions brought regularly from Ostia and other neighboring towns; that the price of grain was fixed at a very low figure; and that admirable regulations were made for rebuilding and avoiding a recurrence of the disaster. There was never any complaint that Nero did not do all that could be done to alleviate suffering after the fire, and while these measures, naturally enough, had no effect in diminishing the public feeling against Nero, they were effective in helping the people whom they were designed to help.

So far only instances of fact have been considered. As to theory, our own age can find little to add. We must still agree with Cicero that nothing appeals more to the best in human nature than kindness and generosity, and that helping the poor is a form of charity which is of service to the state as well as to the individual. The younger Pliny emphasizes the duty of helping others, and of seeking out those who are in need without waiting to be asked. Juvenal regards the capacity for sympathy for any human grief or trouble as Nature's greatest gift to man. " What good man," he says, " can believe that the woes of others concern him not? " The elder Pliny says much in one short sentence, " For mortals to aid mortals, is divine." Seneca was constantly preaching the duty of kindness and helpfulness. It is not too much to say that all the principles of humanity and charity which have ever been known are to be found in his writings. His teaching on this subject might be summed up in one of his own terse sentences, *Homo res sacra homini.* Passages similar to those which have been quoted are many, and the evidence indicates that in this period there was an increasing recognition of the duty of human helpfulness.

The time of the Roman Empire and notably the Antonine Age was essentially an age of cities, of highly developed civic life, and throughout all the cities and towns of the Empire there was a strong feeling of civic responsibility as well as of civic pride. Local patriotism, love of the *patria,* as the native town was called, was characteristic of the time, and in many cases this was heightened by rivalries between neighboring towns. There has probably never been any other period when there was such a universal desire to beautify the town, and when there were so many beautiful towns as there were in the Roman Empire. The munificence of individuals often took the form of some gift to the community, and it was not from residents only that such gifts came. Many a small town in the provinces received substantial tokens of interest and affection from its sons who had gone to Rome to live, but who never lost their love for the home of their boyhood. Public buildings of all kinds, temples, colonnades, basilicas, theatres, and various others, were frequently given or restored by individual citizens. Many of the buildings still seen in Pompeii were the gifts of private citizens. The Temple of Fortuna Augusta was given by a certain M. Tullius. The priestess Eumachia and her son erected the building supposed to have been a cloth market, and two of the Holconii supplied the funds for a large part of the great theatre. The Temple of Isis which had been destroyed by an earthquake was rebuilt by a wealthy freedman in the name of his six-year-old son. The elder Pliny tells of two physicians who spent their entire fortune in lavish gifts to the city of Naples. From a vast number of other towns in the Empire, both in Italy and in the provinces, similar evidence may be collected. Casinum had a temple and an amphitheatre given by that very sprightly old lady, Ummidia Quadratilla, of whom Pliny writes in one of his letters. The ruins of this amphitheatre may still be seen near the modern town Cassino. One of the most interesting buildings in Timgad in North Africa is a large market which was given by a man and his wife. At Guelma in Africa a theatre was given by a woman whose name was Annia Aelia. Her name ought to be remembered, for her theatre was restored not many years ago and plays are again given there. The *thermae,* those magnificent establishments for the name of which the common translation "baths" is ludicrously inadequate, were frequently given or restored by private citizens.

In some of these gifts of buildings, as in public buildings at all times, the money may have been unwisely spent; but the gift of a good water supply cannot fail to be a blessing to any town, and one of the most common benefactions was the building or repairing of aqueducts and fountains. If anyone reflects upon the great abundance of aqueducts in the Roman Empire, and the long distances from which in many cases pure water was brought, he will be inclined to agree with Pliny that " the world has produced nothing more wonderful."

Generous contributions were often made also by individuals for works which were of service to the public, but which by their nature could not be permanent. The man who repaired pavements and built steps for the use of the community must have been blessed by his contemporaries, and although he may have been forgotten after the steps were worn out and the pavements needed repairs again, yet the record of many such donors has survived to be read to-day in the inscriptions.

In connection with the subject of buildings it is interesting to notice that in the time of the Empire there was a care for the preservation of monuments, the buildings and all other relics of the past, similar to that which prevails in Italy to-day. Traffic in antiquities was denounced by the Code as " foul and shameful." Some of the modern associations in Rome, *Gli Amici dei Monumenti*, for instance, *Alma Roma, Roma Salus,* and others, might well have had their counterpart in the Rome of the Empire.

To the cause of education we find both the government and private citizens contributing. One of the best known letters of the younger Pliny tells of the founding of a school at Comum, his birthplace, the money for which was to be raised by private subscriptions. Pliny showed a true appreciation of the value of a school to the community, when he said to the fathers whom he was inviting to contribute, *Nihil honestius praestare liberis vestris, nihil gratius patriae potestis.* It will be remembered also that it was Tacitus, one of the most eminent and one of the busiest men of the day, whom Pliny asked to undertake the work of finding teachers for this school.

It is well known that Vespasian, that rough soldier Emperor who made no claim to any literary culture himself, was the first to give a fixed endowment to professors of the liberal arts. Thus he is perhaps to be regarded as the founder of the public system of education which survived until the end of the Western Empire and exercised a profound influence on Roman life. It soon came to be recognized that the endowment of liberal studies is, to quote the words of Symmachus, " a mark of a flourishing commonwealth."

Another form which the munificence of individuals sometimes took was the gift of a public library. The younger Pliny gave a library to his native town together with a fund for maintaining it. The library at Ephesus, which was built early in the second century, was a gift to the city in honor of the donor's father who had been proconsul of Asia. At Timgad in Africa there is an interesting library. When this building was first discovered, its purpose was not known, although it was evidently a public building. Several years later a broken inscription which was found in three pieces, in three different places and in three different years, showed that it was a library which had been given to the town by a public-spirited citizen. Dill, the author of the book on Roman Society quoted above, in commenting on the fact that " the main characteristics of human nature remain fixed from age to age, while the objects of its love and devotion endlessly vary," makes this remark, " We may well believe that the man who in the second century built a bath or a theatre for his native town, might possibly, had he lived in the fifth, have dedicated a church to a patron saint, or bequeathed his lands to a monastery." To this, the reader may feel inclined to add, that if this man had lived in the twentieth century instead of the fifth, he might have done precisely what he did in the second. The man who in the second century gave a library to his native town would certainly have made the same gift in the twentieth. The public libraries of the Roman Empire are a most interesting subject for study, and a subject of which much more may now be learned than was possible even a few years ago.

The public banquets which have already been noticed were a very common form of showing good will to the community. Such banquets were given on various occasions, in connection with the dedication of public buildings for instance, or in celebration of some important event in the donor's family. Another form of gift to the community was that of games and spectacles of various kinds. Many of these were, from our point of view, ill advised, and it is interesting to find that many of the Romans recognized the evils quite as clearly as we do.

No one could examine the inscriptions which bear on this subject without noticing how frequently the names of women appear among the donors. The independent position of Roman women in the time of the Empire is well known, and the inscriptions show that they were in no respect behind Roman men in public spirit.

The number of gifts made in memory of the dead is very noticeable also. Some of these gifts were very similar to those of modern times, memorial chapels, for instance, being very common. Money was sometimes given also for other purposes which to modern ideas seem less appropriate as memorial gifts, but in them all the spirit was the same. That spirit which prompts the memorial gift, whether in the time of the Roman Empire or in the twentieth century, is the desire to do something for the public in memory of the departed.

The numerous benefactions of the younger Pliny are well known, and what Dill says of him is very true. " He had a conception of the uses and responsibilities of wealth which, in spite of the teaching of Galilee, is not yet very common. Although he was not a very wealthy man, he acted up to his principles on a scale and proportion which only a few of our millionaires have yet reached." And Pliny was not exceptional in this respect, as hundreds of inscriptions prove. There probably never was a time when the duties of wealth were so enforced by public opinion, or when these duties were so willingly accepted and performed. There has seldom been a time, as Dill says, when " wealth was more generally regarded as a trust, a possession in which the community at large has a right to share." And there has never been a time when public spirit and liberality on the part of individuals has been more generously recognized by the community at large. We should always remember how many of these gifts by generous citizens, public buildings, banquets, festivals, and various others, were enjoyed by all the people of the town alike, high and low, rich and poor, bond and free. Moreover this spirit of giving, this interest in the community and the desire to do something for it, was by no means confined to the wealthy. On the contrary, it seems to have been almost universal, even on the part of people who had very little to give. This desire was so common that

Martial's assertion that he would like to have money, not for himself, but *ut donem*, ought to be accepted as sincere. There were
many people who recognized the truth of Martial's words, " the
wealth that you give away, is the only wealth that you will always
have." Many people whose means were very small gave something
to the community, and there is a certain pathos in the very insignificance of some of the gifts and benefactions recorded. There
is a pathos too in the design of the donor that the advantages of
his gift should go on forever. The words *in perpetuom* occur so
frequently! But though buildings have crumbled and funds have
vanished, the spirit of giving is going on *in perpetuom*, and even
to-day in reading of the benefactions, whether large or small, of
great numbers of men and women, many of whom are unknown
outside of their own little communities, and whose names mean
nothing to us, we can still honor the public-spirited citizens and
generous givers of an earlier age.

A GREEK SATIRIST OF THE ROMAN EMPIRE

OF all the Greek writers of the Roman Empire the Syrian Lucian is the most outstanding figure. He is moreover one of the most original of the authors of all periods, a real literary genius who in certain lines has never been surpassed. Lucian is commonly spoken of as a satirist, and he was a satirist but he was also more than that. He was a humorist, he was a comedian, and he was an admirable story-teller. He was one of the most versatile of writers and there is such variety in his works that it is impossible to find any one word that describes him accurately. Satirist, while not sufficiently inclusive, is not altogether unsatisfactory, for aside from the satiric dialogues many of his works, whatever their form, have little touches of good-humored satire. But Lucian, although he was a satirist, was not a reformer. He had no delusions as to being able to effect any great change in human society, he did not expect to make the world over. Human folly he found amusing rather than embittering. There is in his writings none of the *saeva indignatio* that characterizes Juvenal, although he does sometimes try, as Horace did, *ridentem dicere verum*.

In Lucian's life there was as much variety as in his works. The exact dates of his birth and death are unknown, but he was a contemporary of Marcus Aurelius and probably lived from about the year 125 to about the year 180. Although he was a Syrian by birth he spent the greater part of his life in Greece. When a very young boy he was apprenticed to an uncle who was a statuary, but stayed with him only a short time and after that he had various experiences and vicissitudes. He studied law and practised for a little while, then gave that up and became a public lecturer. In that profession he travelled extensively and had great success, not only in Greece but in Italy also and in Gaul. Finally he settled in Athens as his home and it was there that most of his works were published after they had first been presented in the form of lectures.

The variety in the works of Lucian is so great that it is difficult to classify them, but the satiric dialogues are the most individual.

Lucian may be called the inventor of satiric dialogue and it is something in which he has never been surpassed. Of these dialogues the three on philosophy and philosophers are among the best known. These are *The Symposium, The Sale of Creeds,* and *The Dead Come to Life.* Lucian's dialogues were not written to be acted, but to be read. They are however so vividly presented that the reader seems to be actually seeing and hearing rather than reading them.

The Symposium presents a company of philosophers gathered together at a wedding banquet. Representatives of the most important schools had been invited, and there was also a Cynic present. He had not received an invitation, but he did not let that prevent his going. The table conversation begins with a dignified discussion of philosophical creeds, but as each philosopher becomes more and more intent in urging his own theories, they all lose their tempers, the discussion degenerates into wrangling, and finally they come to blows. The end of the discussion, and also the end of the banquet, is brought about by the timely overturning of the lamp-stand. The story is related by one of the guests who was not a philosopher himself, and he remarks that it is " not safe for a man of peace to dine with such learned men."

In *The Sale of Creeds* we are present at an auction in which the various philosophical creeds, represented for the most part by their founders, are offered for sale by Zeus, with Hermes serving as auctioneer. The scene of the auction room is very vivid, and the dialogue throughout is lively and full of humor. A question is put to the Stoic in regard to the fees which he charges for his teaching. He replies that all men may be divided into two classes, the receptive and the disbursive. He trains his pupils to be disbursive, but he himself, as far as fees are concerned at least, is receptive. From one philosopher we learn that the difference between men and gods is that men are mortal gods and gods are immortal men. The buyers are of some interest and also the prices paid for different creeds. Pythagoras is purchased by a syndicate and Stoicism by a dealer. Aristippus cannot be sold for he is such an expensive luxury that no one can afford him. The highest price is paid for the Academic, the creed to which both Socrates and Plato contribute. This creed is sold for more than two thousand dollars, while poor old Diogenes is disposed of for about six cents, with the implication that the auctioneer would have been perfectly willing to give him away. The Skeptic is bought very quickly for the buyer says that he will take him first and ask his questions afterwards. The Skeptic of course doubts everything including his own existence and the existence of the man who has bought him. It is to be noticed that although Lucian himself was an agnostic, or more of an agnostic than anything else, he has no more respect for the Skeptic philosophy than for any of the others. The Cynic creed is recommended as being very easy to follow, since it requires neither learning nor any high degree of intelligence to be a Cynic.

We can well understand that this *Sale of Creeds* aroused great indignation in Athens. People thought that Lucian had ridiculed the most ancient and honorable doctrines and had treated with scorn the most famous philosophers. There was such violent denunciation of the author, such a storm of protests that Lucian found it necessary to make some reply. This he did in another dialogue entitled *The Dead Come to Life*. The dead who came to life were the ancient philosophers themselves who were so incensed by the *Sale of Creeds* that they were given permission to leave Hades for one day and go back to Athens to wreak vengeance on Frankness, as Lucian calls himself. Socrates appears first shouting to the others, Plato, Chrysippus, Diogenes, Epicurus, Aristotle, Pythagoras, and Aristippus, to " pelt the scoundrel with plenty of stones." There are little touches in this dialogue now and then which recall some of the comedies of Aristophanes. Frankness has a narrow escape from death, but finally persuades the infuriated philosophers to let him have a legal trial with philosophy herself as judge. The trial is held on the Acropolis and is conducted with much formality. When Lucian is asked his name, he replies that it is " Frankness, Son of Truthful, Son of Renowned Investigator." As to his profession, he says that he is a " bluff-hater, cheat-hater, liar-hater, and vanity-hater." This is exactly what Lucian really was, an intense hater of all sham and pretense. Philosophy remarks that he seems to have a hateful profession, and Frankness explains that there is really another side to it, for he is also a " truth-lover, beauty-lover, and simplicity-lover," unfortunately however he gets little practice in that part of his profession because there are so few people with whom he can use it. Diogenes is chosen to be the speaker for the philosophers at the trial, and makes out a strong case against the prisoner. His speech is very long but that of Frankness who pleads his own defense is longer still. His claim is that his ridicule was not aimed at the ancient philosophers but at their unworthy successors, not against the real but the pretended. This plea seems to be decidedly specious at first, for in the *Sale of Creeds* there is no indication of any such respect for ancient philosophers as Lucian now claims to feel. Yet although there is much persiflage and light raillery throughout his defense, it was undoubtedly the sham and not the real that he had been attacking. That, it must be admitted, was not made clear in the first dialogue, but in reality Lucian always could and did distinguish between the genuine and the counterfeit. The result of the trial was that Frankness was acquitted of the charges against him, and the impostors were summoned to stand trial. They failed to appear however and Frankness was then empowered to go about and brand them so that the false could be distinguished from the genuine. He was also directed to crown the true as well as to brand the false, but complained that he had little use for the crowns.

The Double Indictment is another dialogue in which a courtroom scene is represented and Lucian himself is on trial. Lucian had been a rhetorician but turned to the study of philosophy, and then began to use the form of philosophical dialogue for light satire. Two different accusations are brought against him. Rhetoric, personified as a jealous and very angry woman, accused him of having most ungratefully deserted her after all that she had done for him. Dialogue who might have been expected to defend him also brought accusation against him because he had misused the dialogue form instead of handling it in the conventional way. The piece is very amusing, but it needs to be read entire to be appreciated. The introduction in which Zeus complains of the hard lot of the gods wins the reader's interest at once. " Confound the philosophers," he says, " who say that bliss is to be found only among the gods. If they knew what we endure for the sake of men, they would not envy us our nectar and ambrosia." He then goes on to tell how overworked all the gods are and he himself has more to do than anyone else, because he has to watch all the others. And all this work the gods are doing out of love for men, but it is impossible to escape criticism, for men are never satisfied. Then he says that some lawsuits are to be taken up that morning many of which have been filed away for a long time because the gods have been so overworked that it has been impossible to attend to them before. A session of court is then opened with Justice presiding, and several other cases are tried as well as those against Lucian. The jurors are drawn from the entire body of Athenian citizens and the number varies in different trials. The two suits against Lucian are listed in the court records as " Oratory versus the Syrian," the charge being " neglect," and " Dialogue versus the Syrian," in which the charge is " abusive treatment." The speech of Oratory is especially interesting because it recounts much of Lucian's actual career. That speech is very long, while that of Dialogue is much shorter, because, as he himself explains, it has always been the custom of Dialogue to speak only a little at a time. Lucian speaks in his own defense and wins both cases by every vote but one. It is the same juror who votes against him in both cases and Hermes remarks that voting on the negative seems to have become a habit with that juror.

There are three series of short dialogues, many of them very short, which are among the best known of Lucian's works. These are the *Dialogues of the Dead, Dialogues of the Gods,* and *Dialogues of the Sea.* The *Dialogues of the Dead,* thirty in number, deal with the futility of human life, the vanity of riches, and similar topics. The themes are often trite, but Lucian had the faculty of treating trite subjects in an original way, and some of the conversations between the dead and their guardian deities on the follies of the living are most entertaining. In the *Dialogues of the Gods,* of which there are twenty-six, belief in anthropomorphic deities is attacked and ridiculed, and these were doubtless read with glee by many of Lucian's contemporaries who believed, as he did, that any such belief if at all genuine was due to the most blind and unreasoning superstition, and that in most cases the profession of such belief was not genuine but mere pretence. The *Dialogues of the Sea* are fifteen in number and contain some very charming passages. There is a little satire in these, but it is very delicate satire which rather adds to the charm. The *Charon* also should be noticed in connection with these short dialogues as the theme is very similar to that in the *Dialogues of the Dead.*

Charon, " the grim ferryman," who had seen many souls of men after they had left this world, has his curiosity aroused as to what human beings are, and what they do before death. He therefore asks for leave of absence for a day and goes to Athens. There he meets Hermes on the street and asks him to act as guide. Hermes says that he cannot possibly do it, he has no time, he is really too busy, but he finally consents, for " what can a man do when a friend insists? " After Charon has seen something of what men have to endure in life, he wonders more and more why they should be so distressed at leaving it. Throughout the dialogue there are little touches which indicate that Lucian sometimes felt not only amusement at the follies of human life, but also compassion for its pathos. There are occasional expressions which even recall the attitude of Marcus Aurelius. The whole scene in this dialogue is very vivid. Charon and Hermes are living characters.

Of the dramatic pieces one of the most lively and most interesting is the one which is entitled *Zeus as a Tragedian,* and which might be called *Tragedy in Heaven.* When we begin to read this, we immediately seem to be in the theatre. The program, if there were one, would read as follows: —

> Scene: Heaven.
> Time: The Present.
> Characters (in the order of their appearance):
>> Zeus
>> Hermes
>> Athena
>> Hera
>> Momus (the Spirit of Criticism)
>> Poseidon
>> Apollo
>> Heracles
>> Damis (Athenians)
>> Timocles (Athenians)

When the curtain rises we see Zeus walking rapidly back and forth on the stage, too excited to stand still, muttering to himself, but in such a state of emotion that he cannot speak coherently. Hermes and Athena come in and ask him what is the matter. Zeus replies in verse with a parody on the opening lines of the *Orestes* of Euripides. The *Orestes* begins, " Nothing there is so terrible to tell, no suffering, no disaster sent by God, but poor humanity may have to bear it." Zeus begins, " Nothing there is so terrible to tell, no suffering, no disaster on the stage, that I cannot tell worse." Athena is properly impressed and urges Zeus to go on and tell what has happened, assuring him that he can speak freely for there is no one present but the family. Zeus continues in the same poetic style without telling anything until Hera loses patience and interrupts him saying that she cannot play up to him in that tragedy performance, for she has not swallowed Euripides whole as he has. She adds that she knows perfectly well what the trouble is, simply another of his love affairs. Zeus is indignant at that. " You do not know," he says. " If you did, you would shriek and scream." Hera replies that she would do nothing of the kind, for she never shrieks and screams, and a new love affair never disturbs her now because she is so used to them. Finally Zeus calms down enough to tell what the disaster is. He had been down to Athens and, disguising himself as a philosopher, he had gone into an assembly where a debate was going on, thinking that he might take an academic interest in listening to it. To his horror he found that the question under discussion was whether the gods existed or not. One of the speakers, Damis, an Epicurean, argued that there were no gods, while Timocles, a Stoic, whom Zeus seems to regard as a " good, simple soul," tried to defend them. The meeting was finally adjourned until the next day when the debate was to be concluded and the question decided once for all, and Zeus hurried home in this state of consternation. Even Hera, who had told Zeus in the first place that she saw no reason for his behaving like an actor on the stage, becomes excited now, and thinks that he was quite excusable for ranting. Now the question is, " What shall we do about it? " Hermes proposes to call a meeting to discuss the matter, " the genuine Anglo-Saxon remedy," as one commentator remarks. Athena on the other hand thinks that the less said about it the better. She would like to have Zeus act as dictator and settle the matter himself without any talk. But the others say that there will be much talk about it in any case, and Zeus will be considered a tyrant if he does not present the question to the entire Council of the Gods. Hermes is told accordingly to summon an assembly. When the deities come together Zeus rules that they are to be seated according to the material and the artistic value of their statues. But the question immediately arises as to which of the two shall take precedence. Should not a statue of gold, Hermes says, if made by an inferior artist, take a lower place than a work of Phidias in marble? Zeus says that it ought to be so certainly, but he regretfully admits that nowadays gold takes the first place. Hermes, after declaring that there will be only foreigners, the *nouveaux riches*, on the front seats, begins to arrange the assembly on that principle. But the question of precedence arouses dissatisfaction and disputes among the gods themselves, for most of them are jealous of someone else. The Colossus of Rhodes claims a place in the front row, for he says that although his statue is of bronze it is so large that it cost as much as sixteen gods of gold. He however is requested by Zeus to stand up, because if he sits down anywhere there will be no room for anyone else. Finally after there has been much disputing among the other gods, Zeus in despair tells them to sit down anywhere, and some other day a meeting shall be called on purpose to consider all questions of precedence. This whole passage of which only a small part has been noticed is a delicious burlesque on the difficulty which is often encountered in determining questions of precedence in a large assembly. After the matter of seating has been dropped, there is loud complaint among the gods because the refreshments have given out, and some people, so others say, have taken more than their share. When Hermes is told to proclaim silence, he says that really he does not see how he can, for there are so many of these immigrant deities who do not understand Greek, and he is not enough of a linguist to address them in Scythian and Persian and Thracian and Celtic. He succeeds by a gesture, however, in making them keep still. At this critical moment when silence prevails and all are waiting for Zeus to begin his speech, he has an attack of stage fright, and confides to Hermes that he has completely forgotten the introduction which he had so carefully prepared. He proposes therefore to begin with his famous Homeric introduction, " Attention, all ye gods, and all ye goddesses too! " but Hermes shakes his head at that. Homer, he says, is all out of date, but Zeus might use one of the speeches of Demosthenes with some little modification, " for that is the way most people make speeches nowadays." Zeus welcomes that suggestion saying that

Demosthenes is certainly a great help to any public speaker who
has nothing to say. Since Demosthenes began his speeches with
" Gentlemen of Athens," Zeus begins his with " Gentlemen of
Heaven," and tells them à la Demosthenes that they must " grap-
ple with the issues of the day." But after a few lines in ora-
torical style he says, " Now my Demosthenes fails me," and proceeds to set forth the critical situation in everyday language.
Great is the consternation in the assembly, for the danger was
that if men ceased to believe in the gods, the gods would of neces-
sity cease to exist. An excited discussion follows. The first
speaker is Momus the Spirit of destructive criticism, the per-
sonification of censoriousness. Momus in Greek mythology was
a professional grumbler, always finding fault with everything
that the gods did. He makes a very long speech in this meeting
as is to be expected, for censoriousness can always do a great deal
of talking. He declares that the critical situation is entirely the
fault of the gods themselves, and dwells especially on their negli-
gence and their habit of letting things go and expecting to " pull
through somehow." When Momus has finished his first speech,
the chairman remarks that to reproach and criticize and find
fault is easy, but to show how the situation can be improved is
a very different matter, and that cannot be expected from Momus.
Throughout the whole discussion Momus speaks in opposition
to everything that is suggested. He calls on Apollo to deliver
an oracle and tell them in plain language who is going to win the
debate in Athens. Apollo protests that he cannot do that because
he has no tripod there, nor any of the other essentials for oracle
giving. Finally however he yields to pressure and pours out an
oracle in eight hexameters which is as ambiguous and non-com-
mittal as most oracles were. Poseidon suggests that if the atheist
should be " removed " before the debate begins, that would be a
simple and effective way to prevent his winning it. But Zeus
says with real wisdom that removing the individual would do no
good, if the question itself remained unsettled. Heracles, who
naturally believes in force as the way of settling all questions,
proposes that they all listen to the debate, and if they see that
the atheist is winning, he will shake the building down and thus
dispose of all concerned. After some further discussion it is
finally decided to open all the doors and windows of Heaven so

that the gods can lean out and listen to the debate in Athens, and for this purpose Zeus orders the Hours to drive away all clouds so that their view may be unimpeded. With these preparations the first act, as we might call it, closes.

In the second part there is a dialogue within the dialogue. The scene on the stage is the assembly at Athens where a hot debate is going on between the two philosophers in the presence of a large audience. With a little imagination we can also see far up in the sky, a little dim perhaps, but visible, the hall of the gods with the deities craning their necks out of all the windows, listening to the debate and making comments upon it. Zeus is very anxious, for he recognizes that Damis the atheist is much more able in debate than Timocles, the defender of the gods, and says in a tone of resignation that all they can do for the latter is to pray for him. In the debate Timocles uses very abusive language, and Zeus says that he should be encouraged in that for it is his only strong point. His arguments, so Zeus declares, are such commonplace, everyday arguments that they are easy to overthrow. Some of the comments of the gods on this debate in regard to their own existence are very racy. Momus makes various remarks which are very much to the point although they are not helpful. The defender of the gods is hopelessly defeated in the debate, but since he will not admit his defeat, no harm is done. As Hermes remarks to his father, quoting a verse of Greek comedy, " Nothing have you suffered, if nothing you admit." Zeus however has great respect and admiration for the atheist and thinks that there would be some hope for the gods if they could have him as their champion.

Among Lucian's works there are essays several of which are somewhat didactic in character. There is one on slander which, although it is rather trite and commonplace for the most part, is of interest because it gives a very vivid description of an allegorical painting representing slander by the Greek artist Apelles. This description is so detailed that it indicates that Lucian had himself seen and studied the painting, and that his article was inspired by it. His description moreover is of special interest because it evidently inspired Botticelli's painting of the same subject. The painting of Apelles is no longer in existence, but that of Botticelli may still be seen in the Uffizi in Florence, and it is interesting to compare the figures which are seen in this picture with those of which we read in Lucian. There are other indications in Botticelli's works that he was familiar with Lucian, and Lucian's influence may be seen also in the works of other artists. There are other themes in Lucian too which seem to have been inspired by works of art, some of those in the *Dialogues of the Sea,* for instance. Although Lucian's references are for the most part only incidental, they show such keen observation as to justify Gardner's statement that he was " the most trustworthy art-critic of antiquity." It may be that his early work in sculpture developed, or began the development of, a keenness in observation and a critical faculty that he would not have had without it. It is now well known that the making of collections of works of art is by no means a modern invention, but something that had become common long before Lucian's time. Throughout the Roman Empire there were temples rich in such collections, and Lucian in his extended travels had doubtless seen many of them.

The Ignorant Book-Collector is a diatribe against a man who expects to gain a reputation for learning by collecting books and boasting of his library. Lucian compares him to the tyrant Dionysius who expected to improve his literary style by writing on tablets that Aeschylus had used. Such a collector, knowing nothing about books himself, is entirely dependent on what he is told, and he is often ludicrously misinformed. He hears " old books " spoken of as treasures, but as he does not know the difference between books valuable for their antiquity and those that are worn out, he pays a high price for worthless books simply because they are in poor condition. This invective is decidedly bitter and seems so personal that it is thought to have been directed against some personal acquaintance of Lucian. That is entirely possible, but it is also possible that he had more than one person in mind, for ignorant book-collectors are to be found in every age.

There is an essay entitled *My Native Land* which is about what one would expect from the title. It is not especially characteristic of Lucian and we might never have thought of him as the author if it had not come down to us under his name. Yet there is no reason why he should not have written it and it is probably one of his genuine works. He makes one remark that is always true, " Those who get on badly in foreign countries are continually crying out that their own country is much better."

The Dream is one of the best known of Lucian's works because it gives a certain amount of autobiography as well as fiction and is the source from which many of the known facts in regard to Lucian's life are learned.

There is a little skit on the absurdity of some of the prayers and sacrifices offered by human beings in the hope of winning divine favor, as if men thought that the blessings of the gods were for sale rather than to be given away. In this, various mythological tales are rehearsed in such a way as to make them utterly ridiculous.

Another, entitled *The Lover of Lies* or *The Doubter,* tells of a conversation dealing for the most part with the supernatural. In form this resembles the *Symposium,* being not a dialogue but the account of a dialogue. One man tells another of a conversation in which he himself had taken part, and tells it in great detail repeating what he himself had said and what other people said. This conversation sounds very natural, for we have all heard similar talks in which one person after another tells what may come under the general head of " ghost stories," extraordinary occurrences for which no explanation can be found. Many such occurrences in every age seem to be well authenticated, and many people find it entertaining to listen to such stories, even those who have no belief in a supernatural cause. Lucian refers also to some of the fabulous tales told by guides to gullible foreigners, and remarks that if there should be a law against the telling of such stories in Greece, the guides would starve to death, for tourists would not pay so much for hearing the truth. There are various references not only in Lucian but in other authors also to guides very similar to some of the guides who are to be seen to-day in both Greece and Italy.

Another interesting passage in this article tells of how the friends who were calling on a man who was ill all had remedies to suggest to him. Most of these were utterly absurd, but they were listened to with great interest by people who had no respect for the doctor's advice because it was too simple. He said that all the man needed was to abstain from wine and have a light diet for a time.

There is a short article which sets forth the humiliations endured by some of the educated Greeks who accepted positions in the households of wealthy Romans, willing to submit to anything because of the high salaries paid, or at least expected. There was so much of this in Lucian's time that many people regarded it as one of the evils of the age, and Lucian makes an earnest protest against it.

The Professor of Public Speaking is a satire in which Lucian is very serious in thought as well as very satirical. It is an attack on the new fashion in oratory which prevailed in the latter part of the second century, and on some of the new theories in regard to making education easy. Many people complained that the traditional course of training was too arduous and time-consuming. They wanted an easier way. Lucian therefore presents in this article a professor who offers a short cut to fame as an orator, and assures his pupils that anyone who thinks that hard work is essential to success is entirely behind the times, an old fogey. Ignorance, he says, is an advantage, and recklessness most useful. He advises his pupils to have a list of catch-words on hand for they can always be resorted to when you don't know what to say. Obscure and unfamiliar words also he recommends because they give a learned sound to a speech, and he tell his pupils that what a speaker says is not of so much importance as it is to keep on talking. " As for reading the classics, don't do it." Why waste time on the works of " dead men of a by-gone age? " Lucian's professor evidently had an opinion of the classics not unlike that held by some people at the present time.

Another essay which is full of satire is entitled *How to Write History*. This was written just after the Parthian War which seems to have inspired as many people with the desire to write about it, both the war itself and its causes direct and indirect, as the World War of recent years. The number of books published was very large and many of them, like many of the recent books referred to, were too hastily thrown together to be of any value. There was a real epidemic of history writing at that time, Lucian says, and he himself caught the fever. His subject however was not history but history-writing, and under this title he makes very keen and witty criticisms of some of the works in circulation. He sets forth the ludicrous mistakes in geography made by authors who were in too much of a hurry to look up the location of places of which they wrote, and as an illustration of exaggerated statements which were very common in these works he quotes an author who described a battle in which he said seventy-two thousand of the enemy were killed while the Romans lost only two. He refers also to an author who tried so hard to imitate Thucydides that he became more Thucydidean than Thucydides himself. Someone has said that this work might have been entitled " How Not to Write History," and that is true of a large part of it. The author of a history that is worth while, Lucian says, must be independent in his judgments, fearless and incorruptible, " not afraid to call a fig a fig and a spade a spade " and capable of stating facts without considering what people will think of them.

Eighty-two works have come down to us under the name of Lucian. Of these a few have been rejected by most scholars as undoubtedly spurious, and there are several others the authenticity of which has been questioned. There are probably however at least sixty which should be accepted as genuine. Of these it is difficult to decide which ones to choose for consideration in a short article, and it is safe to say that no two people would make exactly the same selection. There is one however which no one would omit, and that is the True Story. Although it is for skill in satiric dialogue that Lucian is best known, his skill in narration is hardly less. That would be evident from the short narrative passages in other works even if we had nothing more, but the True Story is all narrative. This is a story of adventure and it contains parodies of marvelous tales which are found in Greek literature of all periods and many of which were written in Lucian's own time. He says in his introduction that he would mention these works by name were it not that his readers would easily recognize them without the titles. Unfortunately many of these works have been lost and the modern reader therefore must inevitably in many cases lose the force of the parody because of not knowing what is parodied. One of the works to which reference is made was a description of India written by a man who had " never seen India or even heard of it from anyone with a reputation for truthfulness." There seem to have been many other accounts also of remarkable journeys which had taken place only in the imagination of the authors. Lucian says that he does not criticize these authors for making untrue statements, " because that was such a common practice among philosophers," a dig at Plato's *Republic* probably. By reading some of these stories of travel and adventure Lucian became inspired, so he says, with the desire to hand down to posterity some narrative of this kind, and since he had not done anything worth writing about, he would write about something that he had not done. Then after telling his readers that nothing in the *True Story* is true, he proceeds to write the account of a journey which exceeds in marvels everything that had been written before it, and which no imitator or writer of similar stories in later times has ever been able to surpass. It has sometimes been compared with *Gulliver's Travels,* but it has none of the bitterness of that work. The *True Story* is ludicrous, absurd, overflowing with rollicking fun, but it is never bitter. The story is told in the first person. Lucian says that he and fifty companions chartered a ship, engaged the best sailing-master to be found, stored the ship with an abundant supply of provisions and set out on a voyage of exploration, eager to learn where the end of the ocean was, and who lived on the other side. Early in the voyage they encountered a heavy storm which lasted for seventy-nine days, but on the eightieth day it abated and they came to an island where they landed. There they found an inscription which stated that Heracles and Dionysus had been on the island. The travellers might have distrusted the genuineness of the inscription, for inscriptions can always be forged, but they also saw some footprints the size of which indicated Heracles. And when they came to a river of wine, they knew that Dionysus had undoubtedly been there. The fish in this river were intoxicating and Lucian speaks of them as edible wine. Soon after they went on board again and left the island, they encountered a whirlwind. This was so powerful that it lifted the ship right out of the ocean into the air, and in the air it was whirled along for seven days and seven nights going higher and higher until they came to the moon where they anchored. They set out to explore the moon but were soon arrested as being suspicious foreigners. That was alarming, but fortunately Endymion was King of the Moon, and when they were taken into his presence, he immediately recognized them as Greeks and gave them a cordial welcome. It was a time of great stress and excitement in the moon, for the

Moonites were planning to colonize the Morning Star, and the Sunites "out of pure jealousy" had declared war and a battle was expected the next day. The travellers enlisted in the army of the Moonites and took part in the battle of which Lucian gives a vivid description. The signal for the battle to begin was given by the braying of donkeys, for on both sides they had donkeys as trumpeters. The account of the battle is very thrilling, and the contest ended by a complete victory of the Sunites who built a solid wall of cloud in the air so that the rays of the sun could no longer reach the moon. That made the Moonites eager to come to terms as soon as possible, and the treaty of peace is a document quite worth reading. The Moonites among other conditions imposed upon them agreed to let anyone who chose take part in colonizing the Morning Star, and to allow all the stars to have home rule. A commentator on Lucian would probably compare this treaty with the one made by the Athenians and Spartans as recorded by Thucydides, but it might also be interesting to compare it with certain treaties of more recent times. Many marvelous things are related of the customs and peculiarities of life in the moon, and any reader who does not believe these accounts is invited to go to the moon himself and see if they are not all true.

When Lucian and his companions finally returned to the sea, they were very glad to be back on the water again after the long voyage in the air. But their joy was short-lived, for they were soon swallowed ship and all by an immense whale, a whale " at least a hundred and fifty miles long." Then follows a long account of the life inside the whale where they stayed for a year and eight months. They finally managed to escape by steering the ship through one of the interstices between the creature's teeth. It used to be supposed that this story of the whale was a direct parody on the Jonah story, but it is now known that there were other versions of that tale long before Lucian's time. The next port where they landed was quite different from anything they had found before, for on this voyage they reached the Isle of the Blest where Rhadamanthus was both king and judge. Lucian and his companions arrived at a time when various trials were going on of people who had recently died, and they themselves were arrested and brought before Rhadamanthus on the charge of going to the Isle of the Blest while still alive. That was contrary to all precedent, but the case presented difficulties because it was also contrary to all precedent for anyone who was still alive to be judged by Rhadamanthus. After careful consideration of the matter and consultation with other authorities, including Aristides the Just, it was decided that after they died they should be tried on the charge of excessive curiosity, but that in the meantime, since they were already in the Isle of the Blest, they might remain for a time but not more than seven months. Then follows a long account of the wonderful time they had there. There is a detailed description of the city with its foundations of ivory and its buildings of gold, of the table in the Elysian fields where the couches are of flowers, the winds serve as waiters, nightingales and other birds bring flowers and drop them on the tables as they sing. At the tables the guests enjoy poetry and song, especially the epics of Homer who is present himself together with Odysseus. Near the table are two springs, one of Enjoyment and the other of Laughter, and from these they all drink and the feast goes merrily on. Lucian tells also of many of the people whom he saw in the Isle of the Blest. The list includes names famous in history, legend, and mythology, who appear all together. There were the veterans of Troy, the Italian Numa, and the Persian Cyrus, Alexander and Hannibal, Lycurgus of Sparta, and Socrates, and many others. It is interesting to notice also who were not there. Plato was not in the Isle of the Blest because he was living in his own imaginary city under the constitution and laws that he wrote himself. Nor were there any Stoics there, as they were still climbing the steep hill of virtue, but Diogenes had so reformed that he was admitted. It was said that the Academicians wanted to go, but were unable to do so because they were still debating as to whether the Isle of the Blest actually existed or not. Moreover they were unwilling to be judged by Rhadamanthus because they themselves had abolished all standards of judgment. It was said also that many of the Academicians had started to go, but were unable to arrive because of the constitutional inability of Academicians to arrive at anything. Lucian had a long talk with Homer and asked him many questions. Since there were so many theories as to Homer's birthplace, seven different cities claiming that honor, Lucian inquired first of all where he was born. Homer told him that all the theories were incorrect for he was really not a Greek at all but a Babylonian. He told him also that he was the author of all the spurious verses, so-called, in the Homeric poems. Lucian also learned that Thersites, " the ugliest man who came under the walls of Ilium," had brought a charge of libel against Homer, but Homer won the case. Probably as soon as the judges saw Thersites they knew that all that Homer had said about him was perfectly true. Then follows an account of the " Games of the Dead," which included both athletic contests and a competition in poetry. In this Lucian says that Homer was by far the best, but Hesiod won, a covert allusion perhaps to the many competitions of all kinds in which the best is not the one who wins. Soon after the Games were over there was great excitement and consternation because the shades who were confined in the place of the wicked had burst their bonds, overpowered their guards, escaped from their prison, and in great numbers were invading the Isle of the Blest. A fierce battle followed in which the heroes of the Trojan War served as leaders, Achilles being especially prominent. But Socrates also did valiant service for which he afterwards received as a reward a large park in the suburbs. This he named the Academy of the Dead and used to gather his companions there for Socratic dialogues. In the battle the wicked shades were finally driven back and completely defeated, and Homer wrote a stirring account of the battle which he gave to Lucian to take back to Greece. The poem began,

This time tell me, O Muse, of the battle of heroes dead.

The reader is shocked to learn that Lucian was so careless that he lost this poem, and therefore the latest authentic work of Homer has never been published. After a time the Greeks were sent away from the Isle and Lucian was very sad. He cheered up however when he was assured that he would soon return to stay permanently. When he went away Odysseus, without Penelope's knowledge, gave him a letter to take to Calypso. She was much affected by this letter and asked many questions about Odysseus. " To these questions," Lucian says, " we gave her such replies as we thought would please her."

After leaving the Isle of the Blest the travellers saw a little of the Isles of the Wicked and learned that the severest penalties are inflicted on those who in this life had written what was not true, Herodotus being especially mentioned as one of these. Lucian says with perfect smugness that his own prospects for the future life are excellent, because he has never written anything that was not true.

The next port of call was the Isle of Dreams in the harbor called Sleep. There was a river flowing by the city which was called the Sleep-Walker, and there were two springs near the gates the names of which were Soundly and Eight-Hours. The dreams themselves differed in appearance and in character. There were some of them whom the travellers recognized as old acquaintances, having seen them long ago at home. These dreams greeted them very cordially and were most hospitable in offering entertainment.

Then follows a series of various disasters. They were attacked by pirates more than once and finally the ship was wrecked and they barely escaped with their lives.

Thus the *True Story* runs on relating one adventure after another, with unfailing imagination, with little satire, no lessons to teach or theories to expound, but full of absurd invention and bubbling over with high spirits. To appreciate the *True Story* it is necessary to read it entire, and it would be impossible to read it without realizing how many of the similar stories in later times in various languages have been inspired by it. The story is not finished. The second book ends with the shipwreck and the author's promise to tell the rest later on, but it was never continued.

It was formerly supposed that Lucian was an opponent of Christianity, because of certain allusions in some of his works which the early Church writers interpreted as slurs on the Holy Scriptures. This interpretation however is undoubtedly incorrect. It is not probable that Lucian himself was sufficiently familiar with the Scriptures to make satirical allusions to them, and it is not probable that the majority of his readers would have recognized satirical allusions even if any such had been made. Lucian apparently did not take any great interest in Christianity, and it is certain that in his genuine works there is only very slight reference to Christians, but while a little pity is manifested for what he considers their credulity, his attitude is in no way unfriendly.

A long chapter might be written on the imitations of Lucian, for they extend all the way from the Byzantine period down to the present time. The *Praise of Folly* of Erasmus for instance recalls Lucian's *Praise of the Fly,* and the influence of Lucian, with whose works Erasmus was very familiar, may be traced also in his *Colloquia* and various other works. One of the earliest imitations of the *Dialogues of the Dead* was that of Fontanelle which appeared in the year 1683, and short *Dialogues of the Gods* were published in a Roman newspaper a few years ago. In these dialogues some of the Olympian deities discussed Roman affairs of all kinds including questions of international importance and the danger of crossing the street in Rome. Two or three of these were so racy that they were almost Lucianic.

The spontaneity of Lucian's writings adds to their attractiveness. He seems to have written when he felt like it, and on the subject that interested him at the moment. The reader will find a certain amount of repetition in his works. That he occasionally repeated in a lecture something that he had already said in another lecture but to a different audience, is not to be wondered at. But the fact that the repetitions appear in the published form, shows that the works were not revised for publication. Lucian apparently wrote very rapidly and sometimes contradicted himself, but that did not trouble him. There is no unity in the works of Lucian. His versatility was too great to admit of unity and his writings are too miscellaneous to admit of definite classification, but the miscellaneous character in itself adds a certain interest to his works. There is a great difference in the interest of different writings, but even in those that might be called almost dull there are occasional flashes of wit and pithy sayings that make the reader glad that he did not omit the article in which they occur, and any reader who simply dips into his works at random is sure to be rewarded.

In the works of Lucian there are no pictures of family life such as we find in the letters of the younger Pliny, and in the correspondence of Marcus Aurelius and Fronto. Nor are there pictures of small-town social life, of which so many are given in the essays of Plutarch. Yet there is in his works a certain indefinable something that makes the reader feel more and more at home in the second century, more and more familiar with the people and the movements and the trend of thought of the time, and realize more and more in how many respects this twentieth century resembles the second.   One thing that becomes very noticeable is that classical Greece seemed almost as ancient, as far away, to Lucian's contemporaries as it does to many people of the present time.

As for Lucian himself, he was as we have seen neither reformer nor moralist.   He wrote for the entertainment of his readers, not for their edification or instruction.   He may sometimes seem rather frivolous, and yet under the frivolous and almost concealed by it there is often a vein of real seriousness.   In some parts of the *Dialogues of the Dead,* for instance, it soon becomes evident that he had more serious thought than appears at first, and more perhaps than he himself would admit.   His scorn of superstition was intense, his detestation of falsehood and hatred of sham amounted to a passion, and one of his principles was that we should never pretend to believe anything that we know in our own hearts we do not really believe.   Lucian is sometimes pessimistic, but his pessimism is seldom depressing because it is relieved by unfailing humor.   He had a keen understanding of human nature, and as a critic of human life he is stimulating rather than depressing.   He sometimes seems a little hard, and yet we find that he is not incapable of sympathy.   In short Lucian might be called a cheerful pessimist and a jolly satirist.   To describe him briefly we cannot do better than to quote again his own words, and say that he was " a bluff-hater, cheat-hater, liar-hater, and vanity-hater," and that he was also quite as much, even if not so evidently, " a lover of truth and beauty and simplicity, and of all that is akin to love."

THE EMPEROR JULIAN

AMONG the existing portraits of Roman Emperors there is one which is of exceptional interest both in itself and for its extraordinary history. This is a marble bust of the Emperor Julian which may be seen in Acerenza, a remote little town in Southern Italy. Acerenza, the ancient Acheruntia, is seldom visited by tourists and has received scant notice in most guide books, but it has a fine Norman cathedral of the twelfth century or earlier which repays a visit even to a town that is difficult of access. And here on the pinnacle of the façade this portrait of Julian stood for centuries. It was like the majestic equestrian statue of Marcus Aurelius on the Capitoline, in that it escaped destruction at the hands of iconoclasts of the Middle Ages because they did not know who it was. The bust which is of colossal size was probably found at the time when the cathedral was built, and as it was supposed to be a portrait of St. Canius, the patron saint, it was given its lofty position on the pinnacle. There it stood and was always called St. Canius from the twelfth century to the nineteenth, when in the year 1882 the French savant Lenormant identified it correctly as a portrait of the Emperor Julian. It is believed that the bust originally belonged to a statue of which nothing more has been found except an inscription noticed below. The early identification as St. Canius is explained by the fragment of an inscription which probably belonged to the pedestal, and which is now in one of the chapels of the cathedral. The fragment contains only the letters — VLIAN —. Since St. Canius had been bishop of Iuliana in Africa, and it was known that his body had been brought into Lucania by the Christians who escaped from Africa at the time of the Mahommedan invasion, it was natural to complete the inscription as follows, *IVLIANensis episcopus*. Thus the Apostate, the man so loathed by the church through many centuries, was suddenly transformed into a martyr and a saint. The error was a fortunate one, for through it a remarkable example of Roman portraiture has been preserved down to the time when it is possible to think of Julian not merely as an apostate, but as a Roman Emperor who was an able general, a wise administrator, a man greatly loved by his friends, and one of the most interesting personalities in history. But while the fragment referred to, if taken by itself, gives a plausible reason for the identification of the portrait as St. Canius, it would seem that no one of those who accepted that identification could have read another inscription which is on a stone built into the outer wall of the cathedral.

REPARATORI. ORBIS
ROMANI D.N.CL.
IULIANO AUG. AETERNO
PRINCIPI
ORDO ACERUNT.

The stone on which this inscription referring to the Emperor Julian may still be seen was doubtless part of the pedestal of a statue erected in his honor by the people of Acheruntia. Another matter which was not noticed in the twelfth century is that the dress is not that of a bishop but the *paludamentum* of a Roman general. The coin portraits of Julian now in existence are not many and, like most coin portraits, differ somewhat from each other. Some of them however are of great interest and bear such a marked resemblance to the Acerenza bust as to leave no doubt as to the correctness of the identification. The portrait is of intrinsic value as a work of art, a work of such vigor and vitality that it is surprising to find it so late as the latter half of the fourth century. It is one of the Roman portraits that could hardly fail to arouse interest in the subject even if we did not know who the subject was.

While Lenormant's identification was accepted immediately, the position of the bust on the pinnacle of the cathedral made it difficult to study and practically impossible to photograph.[1] But a few years ago when some repairs were made on the cathedral, the bust was taken down and is now preserved for what it really is.[2] The bust is not only of intrinsic value as an example of Roman portraiture, it is also of special interest because it is the

[1] Saloman Reinach in the Revue Archaeologique, Vol. 38, gives an interesting account of how he finally succeeded in obtaining photographs.

[2] The author of this article has not been able to learn the exact date, but it was not earlier than 1922.

only authentic portrait of the Emperor Julian in existence. Reinach has proved conclusively that the two statues in Paris to which Julian's name has been given cannot be his portraits. It was also known long ago that the identification was incorrect in the case of a bust once called Julian which is in the Hall of the Emperors in the Capitoline Museum, and of which there are three replicas, two in the Hall of the Philosophers and one in Naples. Ammianus Marcellinus gives a detailed description of Julian's personal appearance which serves to confirm the identification of the Acerenza bust. Julian's character and personality were full of contradictions. He was both a dreamer and a soldier, both a philosopher and a leader of great and victorious armies, both the able administrator of a vast Empire, and a man who loved to lie in the garden and read poetry. No portrait could represent all that Julian was, and in this one at Acerenza it is not the scholar and the visionary that we see, but the victorious general. The face may not suggest the lover of poetry and of nature, but it does suggest the author of scathing satire. We see here strength and the firmness that was such a marked characteristic of Julian and was shown in all that he accomplished or attempted. That the face suggests a man somewhat older than Julian was when he died is not surprising when we remember how strenuous were the last eight years of his life.

It would be hardly possible to give much attention to the portrait without wanting to become acquainted with the life and reign of this young Roman Emperor who lived only a little over thirty years. The whole story reads like a romance, for not only was he so blinded to actualities by his own enthusiasms as to attempt the impossible, but he accomplished much that would have been declared impossible if he had not done it. For many centuries it was so common to think of Julian simply as the Emperor who renounced Christianity, that few people tried to learn anything of his life and reign, of his character and his ideals. But to form a correct idea of Julian one should ignore both the execration of Christians and the exaggerated claims of Pagan admirers, drop both accusation and defense, and try to see him as he really was. That execrations may obscure facts is made evident by the popular conception of Julian which existed from the fourth century until recent times. But execrations cannot change facts and in the twentieth century it is possible to study the life and work of Julian without prejudice and thus realize that although he was an apostate, he was also much more. For learning of his life and character we are fortunate in having the testimony of several of his contemporaries and are not dependent on what later writers have said of him. It is fortunate too that so much of Julian's own writing has survived, for in his writings his personality is revealed. The main sources, aside from Julian's own works, are three authors all of whom knew him personally, Gregory of Nazienus, Libanius, and Ammianus Marcellinus. Of these three writers two loved him and one hated him. The bitter hatred of Gregory was no more intense than was the ardent love and devotion of Libanius. It is a striking fact that two men, both men of superior intelligence, similar in education and culture, coming into contact with one of the outstanding figures of history, differed so completely in their estimate of him. To the one Julian was a paragon of virtue, to the other he was a monster of iniquity. There is no doubt that Libanius and Gregory both believed all that they said, but both were so carried away by the intensity of their own feeling that neither was capable of impartial judgment. Ammianus Marcellinus on the other hand, although his admiration for Julian was no less deep, and his affection for him no less ardent than that of Libanius, was capable of seeing his defects as well as his good qualities. Ammianus in his history presents a very vivid picture of Julian and his account is of special value because of the impartiality of his judgment.

The main facts of Julian's short life can be briefly told and easily remembered. He was a nephew of the Emperor Constantine and was born in Constantinople in the year 331 or 332. His full name, Flavius Claudius Julianus, is seldom heard, although the first and second were names in the Constantine family. The name Julianus came to him from his maternal grandfather who bore that name himself, and it is interesting to notice that Julian seems to have resembled his mother's family much more than his father's. There is very little known of his father, and of his mother, Basilina, we can learn only enough to make us wish that it were possible to know more. One fact of interest is that her love for Greek literature was almost as great as Julian's own. Unfortunately for her child she died only a few months after his birth, but she herself was fortunate in that she did not live to witness the murder of her husband and the other horrors that followed soon after the death of Constantine. It was when the little Julian was only six years old that there was a family massacre instigated by the sons and successors of Constantine who began their reign by putting to death two uncles and four cousins. Julian himself and a brother only a little older were spared because they were so very young. The three sons of Constantine soon quarrelled among themselves and finally Constantius became sole ruler of the Empire. Julian's earliest years were probably spent in Constantinople, and for the most part, it is thought, with the family of his mother. His education was entrusted to a man who had also been his mother's teacher and who often talked to the child about his mother and told him how she had loved the poems of Homer. From this teacher Julian even when a little boy began to acquire that love of Greek literature and Hellenic culture which increased as he grew older until it became an absorbing passion. As a child he used to spend his summers in the country on a small estate which had belonged to his grandmother, where he would lie in the garden, look out over the sea, and read the poems which he had already learned to love.

When Julian was about ten years old he and his brother were sent to a solitary fortress in Cappadocia where they were kept for several years. They were treated as princes to a certain extent, but although the fortress had the luxury of a palace, it was to them a prison. Cut off from the outside world, with no companions of their own age, without friends, the solitary repressed life which the two boys lived here was pathetic. In Julian's case the lack of companionship had the effect of throwing him more and more on his own resources and stimulating his delight in the beauties of nature and in stories of the past. His enthusiasm for Greek literature and Hellenic culture gradually became really religious in its character. Love for the culture of the ancient world and loyalty to religion were in his mind very closely connected.

After about six years of confinement in Cappadocia Julian's brother was recalled to the court and he himself was sent to Nicomedia, the city where Libanius, the most noted rhetorician of the age, was living and teaching. Julian was much attracted by this teacher, and although he was forbidden to attend the lectures of Libanius, he bought those which had been published and read them with avidity. The fact that he was forbidden to hear the lectures doubtless stimulated his interest in them. In Nicomedia Julian came also under the influence of Neo-Platonic philosophers, and Neo-Platonism, really a religion more than a philosophy, was especially attractive to him because of his love of the mystical. After the stay in Nicomedia Julian was allowed, or perhaps ordered, to go to Athens, the city for which he had always longed. He says in one of his letters referring to his being sent to Athens, that others considered him an exile, but he himself felt that he had thereby gained " gold for bronze." The Emperor's plans allowed him to remain only a few months in Athens, but they were among the happiest, and in some respects the most important, months of his life.

Thus we see how Julian's whole education tended to deepen the love of Hellenism which began with his earliest studies. From his very first teachers he became familiar with the high ideals of virtue taught by Pagan thinkers, while at the same time he was seeing something of the vice and corruption which prevailed in the Christian court of Constantinople. A child under such circumstances sees much that he does not understand, but he remembers, and later on he will understand. Much of Julian's opposition to Christianity may be traced to the years of his childhood when, as someone says, he looked at Christianity and Christians " through the blood-red mist of the massacre of his relatives," father, brother, uncle, cousins. Even as a child he heard much of the two factions of Christians who were attacking each other with increasing ferocity. He saw in Christianity a force that caused deeds of fierce cruelty, which apparently sanctioned murder and adapted itself to the vices of a wicked and licentious court, a religion that was characterized by the most bitter strife between those who held the same faith. If the Christians whom Julian had known personally had been of different character, his conception of Christianity would have been very different. To form a just estimate of Julian we must remember these facts, we must remember that " all that was horrible in the life of this sensitive, lonely orphan boy was Christian; while all that was helpful and delightful was drawn from Greek literature."

In the year 355 there came a great change. This young student only twenty-four years old, whose childhood had been lonely and who had lived much of his life in retirement, a scholar and a dreamer, without military training, was suddenly raised to the Caesarship by the Emperor Constantius and sent to Gaul in command of an army. As he himself afterwards said, he felt like a man who had suddenly been called upon to manage a four-horse chariot without ever having learned to drive. But the disaster which might have been expected, and probably was expected, did not come. This dreamy, awkward young student who seemed utterly unfitted for the responsibilities so unexpectedly thrust upon him was all at once transformed into an able general and a wise administrator who was adored by his soldiers and inspired love and loyalty throughout his whole province. The entire period of Julian's public life embraced only eight years, from 355 when he was sent to Gaul, to 363 when he was killed in battle with the Persians. But the story of these years, few though they are, is too long to be touched upon here. Through the death of Constantius Julian became Emperor in the year 361, and it has been well said that for the next eighteen months the biography of Julian is the history of the Empire, for little can be learned of any part of the Empire where Julian was not. Anyone who reads the history of this short reign will find many interesting and romantic episodes. When Julian came to the throne, vice and crime, maladministration and abuses of various kinds were prevalent all over the Empire, and in the Christians whom he knew he saw few examples of Christian virtue.

The great desires with which Julian began his reign and by which he was governed as long as he lived were three: to do away with abuses and institute reforms, to restore Pagan worship, and to emulate Alexander the Great. The second of these desires has been made so prominent in church history that it has to a great extent obscured the others. " Julian the Apostate " is a familiar term to many people who know little of Julian the Emperor, of Julian the Reformer, of Julian the General. Many people would find it hard to understand that it was his very eagerness for reform that made Julian so desirous of restoring Pagan worship. The reforms which he accomplished or at least attempted would fill a long chapter if given in detail. It may be said in general that his legislation was inspired by the desire to moderate and equalize public burdens, to secure justice to all, and to increase the general prosperity. He tried both to diminish the amount required for government and municipal expenses and to prevent the evasion of taxes by those who were best able to meet them. It was his aim to put all citizens, including ecclesiastics, on an equality in regard to municipal duties and to grant no special privileges except for the most cogent reasons. Many Christians to whom special privileges had been granted by Julian's predecessors, without any good reason for it, were as indignant at the withdrawal of these as if there had been an infringement of their rights. But in spite of their violent protests no impartial judge could doubt the justice of such measures. Julian gave much attention to providing for the hearing of difficult cases both in the first instance and on appeal, and since he took a keen interest in legal procedure as well as in securing justice, it is probable that he gave his personal attention to many more cases than the Emperors who preceded him. According to Ammianus Marcellinus unscrupulous advocates abounded, and Julian took special pains to have clients protected from the exorbitant demands and fraudulent schemes of such advocates. He discouraged would-be informers, saying that it was not suitable for an Emperor to be influenced by underhand information. In Constantinople Julian did much for the city. He increased the importance of the Senate, granting it powers and privileges equal to those of the Roman Senate, for he considered Constantinople as far superior to other cities as it was inferior to Rome. In this connection he made the remark, " To be second to Rome seems to me a much greater honor than to be considered the first of all other cities." Julian's own love for Rome was great, although he himself never saw the City. He enlarged the port of Constantinople and he founded a library there which was constantly used until it was destroyed by fire more than a century later. He also made drastic changes in the court at Constantinople doing away with a crowd of superfluous officials who were drawing large salaries but doing no work. This measure naturally caused much dislike of Julian on the part of the parasites who were discharged. Julian's retrenchments and economies were welcomed and praised by many people as being in the interests of the public, while they were criticized by others on the ground that they were unworthy of Imperial dignity.

One of Julian's most important reforms was the reorganization of the Imperial Postal Service. It is well known that communication between different parts of the Empire was carried on and made relatively easy by means of the famous Roman roads. A regular system of transports and couriers was organized, and the expense of maintaining it was borne by the provinces and cities through which the roads passed. In the time of Constantius the granting of free passes by all officials from the highest to the lowest was carried to such an extent that it had come to be a scandal, and private citizens in crowds were travelling at the expense of the municipalities. Julian put a sudden end to these abuses, saying that gratuitous services were equally demoralizing to those who granted them and to those who received them. It was made necessary to have the sanction of the Emperor himself for free passes, and he granted very few. His laws in regard to the postal system seem to have been as effective as they were drastic. In the system of taxation provision was made for exemption in the case of real poverty, and also for certain classes of citizens to whom the government wished to give special encouragement, but the evasion of taxes was rendered difficult. The desire to escape municipal responsibilities and duties was one of the evils of the age against which Julian's legislation was aimed.

In his attempts at instituting reforms Julian sometimes made mistakes and he had the disappointments which many reformers have, for he often met with indifference or even hostility where he had expected sympathy and help. It may be said that he sometimes tried to govern too much, and that his inclination to what his subordinates sometimes called interference was one of his defects. But much that he accomplished in the interests of the state was admirable. In Antioch, a city notorious for its licentious life and for the oppression of the poorer classes, Julian's attempts at reform were especially resented and most bitterly opposed. He doubtless lacked tact in his dealings with the people of Antioch, but it was his austerity, his scorn of luxury and contempt for amusements, and his puritanical ideas that made him especially unpopular there.

To Julian's own mind the most important of all his reforms was the restoration of Pagan worship. This was no sudden freak, but something that he had long hoped to do. When he became Emperor not only was Paganism being oppressed and persecuted, but Christianity was divided into two parties who were attacking each other with bitter hatred. It is a lamentable fact that as soon as Christians ceased to be persecuted they became persecutors, that as soon as Christianity was triumphant it began to be corrupt. Tolerance was a virtue little known in the fourth century, and the impression which was made upon Pagans by the antagonism between different sects of Christians is indicated by a short passage in the history of Ammianus Marcellinus who says that no wild beasts were so hostile to man as Christian sects generally were to each other. It may not always be easy to see Julian's point of view. He had been trained in Christian doctrine, and yet he believed that Christianity had been founded on a false basis. Because of the licentious lives of many of the Christians whom he saw about him, he believed that the recognition of Christianity had opened the door to all kinds of iniquity. Revolted by the bitter strife among those who claimed to be followers of the Christ, and full of enthusiasm for classical learning, he compared the lives of many of the Christians whom he knew with the pure and lofty thought of Pagan philosophy which was to him so familiar and so rich in spiritual meaning. In his study of Greek philosophy Julian seems to have found that which met the needs of his own soul, which Christianity, as he had been taught it and as he saw it exemplified in the lives of Christians, had not done. He became convinced that Christianity was doing great harm, that it was a menace to civilization, that civilization could be saved only if Christianity could be replaced by a religious philosophy which venerated ancient religions instead of scorning them, a philosophy that whatever of error it embraced, was permeated with the idea of Deity. He wished indeed to restore polytheism, but a polytheism reformed and purified and transformed into a mystical symbolism. If regretting history were not futile, we might regret the fact that the Roman Emperor who made Christianity the religion of the state was one who rivalled Nero in the murder of his relatives, and wish that it had not been one of the best of men who tried to restore Pagan worship. Julian's attempt seems strange to the modern mind, and yet it ought to be more comprehensible to the scholar of to-day than it was to his own contemporaries, and in justice to him we should always remember that he was actuated not by caprice but by sincere conviction. In this as in many of his other attempts Julian met disappointment. He had expected that those who were indifferent to Christianity would eagerly embrace the restoration of the older worship, but he soon found that indifference, or even hostility, to Christianity did not carry with it enthusiasm for Paganism. It was more frequently the case that indifference to Christianity meant indifference to religion. Moreover many of those who sympathized with Julian's desire had little hope that the restoration would or could be permanent. This indifferent attitude was much harder to endure than the violent opposition from Christians which he had of course expected. Even his good friend Ammianus Marcellinus who was not a Christian, and who had great admiration for Julian, felt no interest in this attempt which he considered visionary and impossible, the mere dream of a philosopher. It was on the fourth day of February in the year 362 that Julian did what he had long hoped to do, proclaimed religious freedom in the Empire and ordered the restoration of temples. Of his policy toward the Christians after this and of the various laws and enactments in connection with it volumes have been written. One fact to be remembered is that Julian was never a persecutor in the ordinary meaning of the word, and one complaint made against him by Christians was that he did not even give them the glory of martyrdom. The rescript by which Christians were forbidden to give instruction in Pagan literature in the schools aroused much criticism even on the part of some of Julian's friends and supporters. But while that prohibition was probably an error of judgment on Julian's part, the principle on which it was based was sound, namely that a man ought not to teach anything in which he does not believe. When we remember how close was the connection in Julian's mind between Greek literature and Greek religion, it is easy to understand his conviction that when the writings of philosophers and poets were expounded by teachers who wished to refute the ideas expressed in these works, incalculable harm was done. The charge brought against Julian by some ecclesiastical historians that he prohibited Christian youths from attending the schools where Greek literature was taught is wholly false. He distinctly states that his edict referred to teachers only and that students could go where they chose.

For the Jews Julian had a very genuine liking which was rather resented by the Christians. The favors which he granted to the Jews and his plan for rebuilding the temple at Jerusalem has caused some moderns to call him a Zionist.

Julian's campaign against the Persians is difficult to understand. Some authorities would have us believe that his passion for Hellenism blinded him to actual conditions and caused him to undertake an unnecessary and dangerous campaign in the hope of rivalling the victories of ancient Greece. And his judgment failed when after gaining a great victory " by sheer bravado," as it has been said, he suddenly abandoned the enterprise, although if he had pushed on he could probably have taken the Persian capital.

Then comes the last episode of this short life. In battle with the Persians Julian was wounded by a javelin and fell from his horse. At first he did not realize the seriousness of the wound and expected to return to the battle. It soon became evident however that his hours were numbered. His intimate friend Ammianus Marcellinus, who was in the army and probably in the tent with him when he died, gives an impressive and touching account of Julian's last hours, telling how he calmly talked with his friends, distributed his personal possessions among those who were dearest to him, and conversed on the sublime nature of the soul. It is noticeable that in these last hours there was no reference to the religious question which had occupied him so much during his life. The legend that Julian exclaimed with his last breath, " Galilean, thou hast conquered! " did not appear until about a century later and seems to have been without foundation. As to the substance of what Julian did say, we may safely trust Ammianus, and one sentence especially in which he thanked the " Everlasting God " that his end had not come by treachery or long illness may well be remembered as among his last words. He was buried at Tarsus, but the body was afterwards removed to Constantinople.

Thus Julian died, a man only a little over thirty years of age,

but one of the most striking figures in the long list of Roman
Emperors. And the freedom of worship which Julian declared,
which Constantine had also declared but soon ignored, perished
with Julian himself not to rise again for nearly fifteen centuries.
Even those who have most execrated Julian could hardly deny
the truth of the epitaph on his tomb at Tarsus which said of him
that he was " both a good king and a mighty warrior."

If Julian had never been sent to the army, if he had never
become Emperor, he would have lived in history as an author
and thinker. Although his life was so intensely active from the
time when he was summoned from Athens to Milan by Constantius, he always remained first of all a student. Literature
which had been his chief interest became his recreation. Where-
ever he was, whatever he was doing, whether in camp or overwhelmed by the cares of state, he always took time, generally in
the night, for study and meditation and writing. Julian was a
prolific author and many, although not nearly all, of his works
are extant. He wrote very rapidly, so rapidly that in his works
the indications of haste are very evident. From the point of
literature the reader finds abundant opportunity for criticism, but
for becoming acquainted with Julian himself and with the customs and tendencies of the age in which he lived these works are
invaluable. The extant works are classified as orations, satires,
and letters. The orations or philosophical discourses are rather
artificial and heavy, and less interesting than the satires and
letters. Of satires there are only two. One of these, *The Banquet
of the Gods,* was written for the Saturnalia in the year 362.
This is for the most part a playful rather than a bitter satire.
It represents Quirinus, the deified Romulus, as inviting all the
Gods and all the Roman Emperors to a banquet. The Emperors
come in one by one and are greeted by Silenus who acts as court
jester and has some joking remark to make to each one as he
arrives. When the entire company is assembled, the Emperors
are called upon to make speeches each in his own behalf, for
Quirinus desires that the one who presents the best qualifications
shall be chosen to receive divine honors. Each Emperor therefore
states what his chief purpose had been during his reign, what his
guiding principle was. The whole scene is vividly presented and
in parts it is very amusing. It shows Julian's intimate acquaint-

ance with history, his complete realization of the past. To him the past was no less real than the present. He felt as well acquainted with men who had lived centuries before his time as with his own contemporaries. To a certain extent this satire recalls some of those of Lucian, but Julian was not so witty as Lucian, nor did he have Lucian's lightness of touch. He was rather too serious for playful satire and some of his jokes are heavy. Of the Emperors Constantine was the one who received the hardest treatment. Julian detested Constantine and is perhaps not altogether fair to him. Circumstances had been such that to Julian's mind the worst sides of Constantine's character were the most prominent, and that this Emperor should ever receive the title of " the Great," would have seemed to Julian supremely ludicrous.

The other satire which is entitled *Misopogon, Beard-Hater,* is a satire on himself written from the point of view of the people of Antioch. In that city Julian's austerity, his very simple manner of life and inclination to asceticism were especially disliked, and many satiric verses had been written about him ridiculing among other things the fact that he wore a beard. In this satire under the guise of ridiculing himself, Julian was really ridiculing and condemning all that was reprehensible in a community given over to luxury, extravagance, frivolity, and licentiousness. Julian's reputation has suffered from this work because so many commentators have lacked a sense of humor, and have taken seriously some of the unpleasant but purely ironical remarks which he made about himself. The reader should remember that this work is ironical from beginning to end, for it is only with that fact in mind that it can be understood.

It is in the letters that Julian most clearly reveals himself. The greater part of these were written during his short reign as Emperor, and the collection includes various edicts and public letters as well as those which belong to his personal correspondence. One of these is a letter to the Senate and People of Athens. When Julian accepted the title of Emperor he sent letters to four cities, Rome, Athens, Sparta and Corinth, defending his acceptance and his break with Constantius, but the one to Athens is the only one which has survived. Julian's love for Athens was so great that he was especially anxious to have the approval of the

Athenians in what he had done. It is noticeable that he seems to think of the Athenians of his own day as if they still had the prestige and the standards of centuries earlier.

Of the personal correspondence there is enough left to show what an untiring letter-writer Julian was. Nearly eighty letters are extant and these are only a small part of all that he wrote. Of these letters some are more interesting than others but many of them repay careful reading for the light they throw on the life of the fourth century as well as on Julian's own character, and his affection for his friends is delightfully evident. There are some letters in the collection which are undoubtedly spurious. One of these addressed to Basil is so utterly unlike Julian both in spirit and in language as to show that whoever wrote it knew nothing either of Julian's style in writing or of his character. There are many passages which show his trust in Deity, his belief in the reality of divine guidance and his complete dependence upon it. One from the Sallust is a good example of such passages, " For it is not probable that anyone who puts his trust in God will be forsaken and left utterly desolate. But over him God stretches his hand, gives him strength and courage, and puts into his mind what he ought to do." In one letter he says that if his reign should be successful, it is to God that the glory would belong, and he exhorts himself to keep calm and endure bravely whatever God may send. His belief in the immortality of the soul is expressed or implied in many places and also his belief that to do one's best is a proof of piety. The prayer with which he closes the hymn to the Mother of the Gods is illustrative of his own spirit, the prayer that asks for all men happiness and that highest happiness of all, the knowledge of the Gods.

Julian has sometimes been compared with Marcus Aurelius, but he lacked the balance of Marcus Aurelius and had none of his judicial spirit. He was no less devoted, but he was less wise, and he never attained to the tranquillity of Marcus Aurelius. Julian was not a hero and yet, as Ammianus Marcellinus says, he was worthy to be ranked with heroic characters. He was not a great man, but he came near being great, or perhaps we should rather say that he was one who might have been great, if he had been a little different. With all his firmness he was sometimes inconsistent, and he sometimes defeated his own purposes. He craved approval, he was eager for popularity, but he not infrequently antagonized when he most wished to conciliate. He was a man who enacted reactionary measures, believing that he was inaugurating a new era. Yet though Julian has sometimes been called a reactionary, he was not really such. He was progressive in spirit, but he realized, as some people of the present time cannot, that change and progress are not always synonymous terms. It has been said of Julian that he could not always be fair to those whom he could not understand. That is very true, but it is true of most people, and eminently true of Julian's critics. He was an Emperor who preferred to be called priest rather than prince, an Emperor who notwithstanding his unfortunate attempt to restore Pagan worship after such an attempt was an anachronism, was characterized by lofty ideals, and was full of enthusiasm for all that is noble. Although he did not believe in Christianity, he had a trust in Deity worthy of the highest Christian spirit. Julian was qualified, and to a greater degree than many of the other Roman Emperors, to make a lasting impress on history, and this he might have done if he had lived longer. As it is, his name has been remembered only to be execrated.

The contradictory tendencies in Julian's character were no greater than the contradictions in his reputation have been. He has been hated by those whose religious zeal was very like his own, by those with whom his inner self would have been in perfect harmony. And he has been admired, applauded, and even claimed as one of themselves, by skeptics whose skepticism he would have abhorred. A man of whom it has been truly said that " duty toward men and trust in God was the keynote of his life," he has been remembered only as the enemy of Christianity.

It is a fascinating subject of study, the character and life of this young Roman Emperor who never saw Rome, " mightiest Rome, beloved of the Gods," as he called it. One may regret that he could not have had a different point of view for seeing Christianity, but to anyone who becomes acquainted with Julian the incongruity of his portrait standing on the summit of a Christian cathedral does not seem so great as it did at first. That his portrait should have borne for centuries the name of a Christian martyr and saint seems less strange when we reflect that Julian with his strong convictions and his religious enthusiasm, if he had lived fifty years earlier, might have been both.

A ROMAN POET OF THE FIFTH CENTURY

THE fifth century of our era is one which historians have avoided. Anyone who tries to learn something of that period will be impressed first with how little is known about it, and second with how much of the little which was once supposed to be known is untrue. Those who write of Roman history have considered the fifth century too late to touch upon, unless in a manner so cursory and perfunctory that for the reader it is more exasperating than enlightening. For the mediaevalist on the other hand the fifth century is as much too early as it is too late for the other. Thus a common idea of that period is that it was a dreary, melancholy time, characterized chiefly by wars and rumors of wars and by the break-up of the Roman Empire. Yet the fifth century was a very important and very interesting period of history, for it was the beginning of the new as well as the closing of the old. It witnessed not only the struggle between Romans and barbarians and the beginnings of the modern nations, but it witnessed also that struggle between Pagan and Christian thought which continued for several centuries after Christianity was accepted as the state religion. This is a fascinating subject and one to which more study will be given in the future than it has ever yet received. The fifth century moreover was a time when there was a widespread interest in literature, when every educated man was a literary critic and a potential author. But although it was a time of literary appreciation, comparatively little literature was produced, and very little has survived. That so little of the writing of the period is still in existence is greatly to be regretted, for the best approach to any period of history is not the reading of books about it but the reading of books which it produced. The fact therefore that so little of the literature of the time has survived gives a unique value to a poem which was written early in the century. It is noticeable that the value of this poem, a value both literary and historical, is not recognized in most histories of Latin Literature where it is generally dismissed with few words and those few, in many cases, are words of condemnation only.

The subject of the poem is the itinerary of a journey from Rome to Gaul which the author took in the autumn of the year 416. Of the author himself very little is known except what is told in the poem and the few facts that can be gathered may be enumerated very briefly. His name was Rutilius Namatianus, and he also had the name Claudius, but whether it was Claudius Rutilius or Rutilius Claudius is uncertain because the only two existing manuscripts differ in the order of the names. We know that he was born somewhere in Transalpine Gaul, but what his native town was is uncertain. One conjecture is that it may have been Poitiers, but Toulouse is more probable. Just when Rutilius went to Italy is also uncertain, but as his father was at one time governor of Tuscany, it seems probable that the son may have gone with him and have been educated in Italy and perhaps in Rome. However that may be, it is certain that he lived in Rome later on and that he held high offices there at different times including the two most important ones of the civil administration, *Magister Officiorum* and Prefect of the City. The dates when he held these two offices are known, the first being in the year 412, as shown by a passage in the Theodosian Code, and the second in 414, as we learn from allusions in the poem itself. These two dates are of some importance as we shall see later. The statement has been made that Rutilius also held the office of Consul, but that is mere conjecture and is probably incorrect, since his name does not appear in the lists of the Consuls of his time.

In the year 416 it became necessary for Rutilius to return to his home in Gaul after what had evidently been a long absence. The poem, the title of which is simply, *His Own Return,* is a detailed account of the journey, with an introduction telling of his great sorrow at leaving Rome. It was originally in two books, but only a small part of the second is extant, so the account as we have it breaks off abruptly.

The history of the preservation of the poem is of some interest. There are only two manuscripts extant, or which are known to be extant, and both these are copies of the same one. The earliest manuscript known was discovered in the year 1493 or 1494 in the monastery of Bobbio. It will be remembered that this monastery had a famous library which in course of time was scattered and the greater part of it is now in the Vatican. Not long after the discovery of the Rutilius manuscript a copy of it was made by a man who afterwards became librarian of the Vatican library, and took the copy with him when he went to Rome. Two copies of this copy were made quite early in the sixteenth century. The original was left at Bobbio where it remained for more than two centuries, but in the year 1706 it was carried away by an exiled French general who was serving in the Austrian army, and what became of it is not known. The copy of the original which was taken to Rome has also disappeared, but the two copies of the copy which were made early in the sixteenth century are still in existence. These four manuscripts then, the one found at Bobbio which has disappeared, the copy of the Bobbio manuscript which has also disappeared, and the two copies of the copy which are still in existence, are the only manuscripts of Rutilius Namatianus which are known ever to have existed. One of these is now in Vienna and for a long time it was supposed to be the only existing manuscript of this work, for it was not until the year 1890 or 1891 that the other was found in Rome. This is now in the library of the Accademia dei Lincei. It is bound with two other manuscripts in a small leather-covered volume, and the writing is very clear. The dedication which is on the back of the cover is to *"Genius,"* and that is of some interest because it probably refers to a verse in the poem in which Rutilius uses the word Genius to indicate the Guardian Spirit of Rome. So we may infer that it is to the Guardian Spirit of Rome that the copy is dedicated. The poem of Rutilius seems to have aroused interest very soon after it was discovered, for the first printed edition was made in the year 1520, a copy of which is to be seen in the British Museum. Three other editions were published in the same century. In the seventeenth century at least four editions appeared, in the eighteenth five or more, and in the nineteenth several were published. Of the later editions it is noticeable that the one by Zumpt, a German scholar, which was published nearly a hundred years ago is still one of the most valuable. In recent years some excellent French and Italian editions have appeared. English scholars for some reason did not become interested in this author as early as those of the continent, for the first English edition, and the only one which has yet appeared, was not published until the year 1907.

After Rutilius had been living in Rome for several years, the state of affairs in Southern Gaul made it necessary for him to return to his early home. He needed to go to look after his property there and he wanted to go to try to be of some assistance to the community, to his fellow-countrymen who had suffered from the invasion of a hostile army. To the general reader that would seem to be an all-sufficient reason for his going. And yet some scholars have exercised great ingenuity in trying to find some hidden cause for his leaving Rome. They have conjectured that he had fallen into disfavor with the government. But there is nothing in the poem to indicate that that was the case, and the attentions paid him all along the route are an argument against that theory. Another conjecture, quite the opposite of the first, is that he had been sent to Gaul by the government on some confidential secret mission. Of that theory it may be said that while it is not intrinsically impossible, there is no reason for believing that it is true. Although so little is really known of Rutilius, the poem makes his personality so vivid that the reader soon begins to feel acquainted with him, and that perhaps accounts for the groundless conjectures and vain speculations about him in which several commentators have indulged. But there seems to be no reason why we should not accept his own statement as telling not only the truth but the whole truth.

In the poem several of the friends of Rutilius are mentioned by name and some of them more than once. With these friends too, as with Rutilius himself, the reader begins to feel acquainted, and with regard to them also there have been many conjectures, but very little is really known. The one thing that we can be sure of is that Rutilius had many friends several of whom were among the most prominent men of the age.

The reason for his leaving Rome and returning to Gaul was indeed a compelling reason. Rutilius really wanted to go, but when he went away from Rome, he suffered that overwhelming homesickness which many other people have suffered on going away from Rome. The poem begins very abruptly with the expression of his great sorrow. One editor thinks that this abrupt beginning indicates that some verses have been lost, but a careful study of the poem gives no reason for believing that to be the case. It is more probable that the abrupt beginning was intentional and indicative of the author's state of mind. Since it is addressed not to any specified individual but to the reader, he is speaking to those who read it to-day just as much as to those who read it first, when he says, " You will wonder, reader, at my hurried return, that I can tear myself away from the blessings of Rome so soon." He had been living in Rome at least four years and probably longer when he wrote that, and so he adds with reference the words " so soon," " What stay in Rome could ever seem long to those who would devote their lives to Rome? Nothing is long that pleases without end." Then continuing the same theme, the joy of living in Rome, he has a variation on the common phrase, " thrice and four times happy." Four times happy, he begins to say, but that is not enough and he continues, " nay happy beyond all reckoning are those whose privilege it is to have been born in Rome. But fortunate too are those others to whom the next highest privilege has been granted, in Latium to have their home." Then he goes on to explain why he must go away. " But it is my lot to be torn from the country that I love, because the Gallic fields, marred by long wars, are calling for their son." Southern Gaul where his early home was had been invaded by Goths and had suffered all that a region does suffer from an invading army. The very springs, he says, the trees themselves if they could speak, would urge him to go. And it is not unwillingly that he goes, because he knows that he is needed there. You can stay away from your country, he says, while it is prosperous, but if it is in trouble and needs you, then you want to go. Thus Rutilius was torn in his heart by two conflicting emotions, a real desire to return to his native Gaul, and overwhelming sorrow at leaving Rome. That is a conflict of emotions which has been felt by countless other people who have found it necessary to go away from Rome during the fifteen centuries that have passed since that day in the year 416 when Rutilius went.

Having decided to go, the next question which Rutilius had to consider was whether to make the journey by land or sea. It is well known that in its earlier centuries the time of the Roman Empire was an age of travel, a time when travel to all parts of the civilized world was both easy and common. As tourists the Romans of the Empire rivalled the Americans of to-day. Travel was never more rapid until the use of steam and electricity, never more comfortable until recent times, and never more secure at any time than it was in the early centuries of the Roman Empire. But in the year 416 after the Tuscan territory and parts of Southern Gaul had been invaded by the Goths, former conditions no longer prevailed in that part of the Empire. Roads were out of order, even those which had not been purposely destroyed by the invaders, bridges were down, and some regions were infested by bands of marauders and highway robbers. Rutilius therefore decided to go by sea, saying in the poem, " For since the Tuscan fields and the Aurelian road have suffered raids by Goths with fire and sword, since woods have lost their homes and streams have lost their bridges, it is better to trust with sails the uncertain sea." Before beginning the account of the journey, Rutilius pauses to address Rome directly in a panegyric which is a spontaneous outburst of deep affection and passionate enthusiasm. This panegyric which is over a hundred verses long includes both history and prophecy, and may be left to consider after the narrative of the journey.

The account of the journey describes in some detail all the places which he sees on the way. It is not written like a guide-book however, but is rather an itinerary such as one might send to an intimate friend and relates various little incidents. He was to sail from Ostia, and he speaks of setting out from Rome, of how he wanted to kiss the very gates when he went through, of the friends who came to see him off and who, as he says, " could not say farewell with eyes dry." One friend, Rufius, a young man whom Rutilius greatly loved and for whose future he had high hopes, went with him farther than any of the others, but finally Rutilius told him that he too must turn back. This Rufius is mentioned again in the poem, as we shall see. When they reached Ostia the weather had changed and a storm was brewing. This soon became so bad that the sailing was deferred, and it had to be deferred from day to day until fifteen days had passed. Some commentators have thought it very strange that Rutilius did not go back to Rome for those fifteen days, but there were very good reasons for his not doing so. In the first place he did not know when the storm began that he would have to wait fifteen days. It was simply waiting from day to day, as it generally is when we are waiting for a change of weather. Rutilius would not have gone to Ostia as early as he did if he had known what the weather was going to be, but after that terrible wrench of leaving Rome had been lived through once, there could have been no satisfaction in returning for a day or two and then suffering the agony of going away all over again.

After the long delay they were finally able to sail on the seventh day of October, and at this point in the poem we learn that a young relative of Rutilius had been staying with him at Ostia. This young man had been sent from Gaul to Rome to study law. The affectionate way in which Rutilius speaks of him, saying that he loved him like a son, and the evident interest with which he is looking forward to the young man's future, make the reader wish that it were possible to know more of him. Whether we do know more of him or not is uncertain, for his name, Palladius, appears twice in later years, first as the name of a Praetorian Praefect, and again as the author of a work on agriculture. As far as the date is concerned, either or both of these might be identified with the relative of Rutilius. But while that identification is possible and not improbable, it cannot be proved. Although we cannot learn more of the individual concerned, this passage referring to a young law student of the fifth century is of interest because it is one of many which show that all through the time of the Roman Empire the best place to study law was in Rome itself. There were famous schools in Gaul for all other studies, but for legal training Rome always took precedence. Rome in the fifth century was still as Sidonius, another Gaul of that period called it, " the home of laws."

In Rutilius' account of his journey we shall notice that he was thoroughly acquainted with the history and traditions of central Italy, as well as with its geography, and we shall notice also that he was a very observant traveller, interested in all that could be seen in the places where he stopped. The ship on which he sailed seems to have been one of a small fleet of which he was virtually in command. He had several attendants or companions with him, but as he mentions no one of them by name, we may know that they were not intimate friends. For the voyage small boats had been chosen rather than the larger merchant-ships which would have been used for a summer voyage, because they could keep near the shore and anchor more easily in case of storm. Since these little boats coasted along the shore, the travellers had views of many places where they did not stop and which could not have been seen from larger ships farther out at sea. It is easy for any-one who is acquainted with Ostia to imagine the beauty of that glorious October morning when, after the long period of storms, the sea was calm and the sky was blue with, doubtless, some of those wonderful cloud effects for which Ostia is famous. And it is easy to follow Rutilius in this sail along the coast as they pass places the names of which at least are familiar to all who know this part of Italy. The enjoyment of Rutilius himself in the beauty of the scenery, and his interest in the human associations of the places which he passed was so great that he imparts to his readers something of his own pleasure. The first place that a modern traveller would notice on this trip, Fregenae, is not mentioned but Rutilius speaks first of Alsium, the modern Palo. It is known that Pompey once had a villa at Alsium, and so did Antoninus Pius, but as Rutilius does not mention either of these villas, it is probable that they had both disappeared before his time. As they sail along the coast they pass great villas, he says, where little towns had formerly been, and they pass Pyrgi which was the port of the old Etruscan town now called Cervetri. Ruti-lius did not land there and since he says nothing of the wonderful Etruscan tombs which make a visit to Cervetri of such interest to-day, we may infer that they were not accessible in the early fifth century. And they were not accessible for centuries after that time probably, for the excavations of modern times began only about a hundred years ago. The first day's voyage brought them to Centumcellae, or Civitavecchia as it has been called since it was rebuilt in the ninth century soon after it had been destroyed by the Saracens. Rutilius describes at some length the very fine harbor there. This port was constructed under Trajan, and the younger Pliny who was staying at Centumcellae with Trajan while the work was going on and so was an eye-witness of the con-struction, gives in one of his letters a description of it which it is interesting to compare with what Rutilius wrote of it. Pliny says that the construction is in itself "worth seeing," and he describes in some detail what the process was. He says that this port which will always bear the name of its great founder will be of vast benefit because it will afford a secure haven to ships on a long stretch of coast which had been harborless before. The recent excavations in the Forum of Trajan have given a renewed interest to all the works of that Emperor, and it is pleasing to see that Rutilius three hundred years later was just as enthusiastic about this port as Pliny was when he saw it in the making. The arrival at Civitavecchia was early enough to enable them to take a drive of three miles to see some famous hot springs which were called the " Springs of the Bull." Rutilius was much interested in folk-lore of all kinds. He liked to hear the local traditions and legends which had come down from the long ago, and he tells several of them in this narrative. The ancient story in regard to these springs near Civitavecchia was that they had been found by the pawing of a bull or, as it was interpreted by some people, by the beneficent action of some deity disguised as a bull. The discovery of the springs proved to be of such benefit to the community that the legend of a miraculous origin was not unnatural. Rutilius says that the place was well worth the excursion to see it, and that it had been made famous by a poem which was attached to the door of the temple near by. Of this temple nothing more is known, but the ruins of the baths which were constructed near the springs, the Aquae Tauri, may still be seen. The party passed the night at Civitavecchia and started again at dawn on the following morning.

In the account of the second day's voyage two ancient towns are mentioned where they did not land, but of which they could see something from the ships. The first was Gravisca, " with its scattered roofs and dense pine groves." Gravisca was the ancient port of Tarquinia and had evidently been falling into decay long before the time of Rutilius. At the present time not even its site is certainly known, and the dense pine groves of which he writes are no longer to be seen. The brief reference to the other town, Cosa, which is mentioned by Vergil as one of the cities which sent aid to Aeneas, indicates that of that town also there was left only, as he says, " unguarded ruins and walls decayed." The site was occupied again in the Middle Ages and survived for a time under the name of Ansedonia. It is not however the remains of mediaeval Ansedonia, but of Etruscan Cosa that give an interest to the site to-day. There may still be seen remains of the polygonal walls of which Rutilius speaks, about sixteen hundred yards in all, which are among the finest examples of such walls to be found anywhere. It may well be that if Rutilius had landed at Cosa, he would have seen little more than is visible to-day. But he must have seen quite as much, and it is to be regretted that he did not land and describe in some detail what was to be seen there in the year 416. Although he did not go ashore he was told, perhaps by one of the sailors, of a local tradition which he says was so absurd that he was almost ashamed to repeat it, namely, that the reason why Cosa had been deserted and so had fallen into decay was that one day all the inhabitants had been driven out in a body by an army of rats. In regard to this Rutilius says that one could sooner believe Homer's stories of the wars of Pygmies and cranes. Going on a little farther they come to Portus Herculis, or Porto Ercole as it is now called, where they land and spend the night, having travelled about fifty miles on the second day. Rutilius was especially interested in this place because he saw there the remains of an ancient camp, that of Lepidus the father of the Triumvir. It will be remembered that this Lepidus when he was consul in the year 78 B.C. tried to rescind the laws of Sulla and overthrow his constitution. Declared a public enemy by the Senate, he marched against Rome, was defeated in a battle near the Mulvian bridge, and fled into Etruria. From Portus Herculis where he had camped he sailed to Sardinia, leaving the camp in great haste. Rutilius says that in the wrecked camp itself they discussed Lepidus, what he had done and tried to do, and his head-long flight from Portus Herculis. He then goes on to refer to the Triumvir and to others of the same family, with the reflection that in Roman history many disasters had come through the name of Lepidus.

On the third morning they start even earlier than they had on the other two, before light this time, and sail around the promontory of Monte Argentario. This course required very skilful steering, for it was necessary for the boats to tack repeatedly and at very short intervals. The island of Igilium, now called Giglio, was seen from a distance, an island where many refugees from Rome had fled when the city was besieged by Alaric a few years before. They passed the mouth of the river Umbro, and Rutilius wanted to land there and spend the night, but the crew were so eager to press on that he consented to do so, much against his own judgment. Then the wind went down when they were a long distance from any town, so they had to camp out on the open beach. He describes how they improvised little tents by using oars to hold the canvas, and how they gathered wood for a fire from a grove near by. Rutilius seems to have rather enjoyed this experience. It may be that he had never before had the fun of camping out.

On the fourth day they start again at dawn although there was still no wind. But as the place where they had spent the night furnished no interest for a longer stay, they preferred to proceed by the very slow process of rowing rather than not to proceed at all. The island of Elba was seen at a distance, and the thought of the iron mines there, mines which have been famous since the time of Alexander the Great, caused Rutilius to indulge in some rather commonplace reflections on how much more useful iron is than gold, with the extremely trite remark that the blind love of gold leads to all evil,

Auri caecus amor ducit in omne nefas,

and more to the same effect. The reader would probably have been spared these moralizings if there had been any wind that morning, for Rutilius remarks at the end of the passage that the reason why he wrote it was that he was so bored. About mid-day they reached Faleria, a harbor of some importance at the time, and landed. There they had the pleasure of being present at a village festival, and many people who have travelled in Italy know how interesting that is, and how the interest is increased if we come upon such a festa unexpectedly as Rutilius did. They saw a rustic procession very similar to those that may still be seen in Italian villages on similar occasions. This festival was in honor of Osiris, it being the day when, as Rutilius says, Osiris "to life restored, arouses the sprouting buds to form new fruits." It might seem strange that such a festival should be openly observed as late as the year 416, if it were not known from the Theodosian Code that in the year 399 the Emperor Honorius had given permission for all the merrymakings connected with Pagan festivals provided there were no sacrifices or public worship. Rutilius evidently enjoyed this whole scene just as any of us would enjoy it to-day. After watching the procession, they strolled through the little village and took a walk in the groves and loitered by some very charming fish-ponds. Their enjoyment of Faleria however was rather spoiled by a very churlish and extortionate inn-keeper. This passage is of interest because in so many accounts of travel in whatever country there is a reference to at least one inn where the service is poor, the food impossible, and the charges exorbitant. Rutilius says of this inn-keeper at Faleria that he made them pay for the sea-weed which their sticks had touched, and complained that he suffered great loss in the water that they drank. They seem to have had an animated discussion and Rutilius evidently told the inn-keeper in very plain language what he thought of him, for he says, " We gave him the abuse that he deserved." This inn-keeper as it happened was a Jew, and Rutilius had become so wrought up over it all that he pauses in his account of the journey to relieve his feelings by a bitter invective against Jews in general. He closes this invective with the wish, and it is to be noticed that it was the very worst wish he could think of, that Judaea had never had the advantage of coming under Roman sway. From the point of view of Rutilius the worst fate for any people between the year 1 and the year 400 of our era was to remain outside the pale of the Roman Empire.

The inn-keeper and the altercation with him had so spoiled Faleria for them that they wanted to go away as soon as possible, and they started at dawn the next morning, although the wind was not favorable. The first place of interest to which they came was Populonia, or rather perhaps the ruins of Populonia. This ancient Etruscan town which had once been of great importance had been destroyed in great measure in the time of Sulla, and by the time of Augustus it was practically deserted, as we learn from Strabo. The desolation described by Rutilius was apparently very much what is to be seen there to-day. Rutilius however had pleasant associations with the place for he received there good news from Rome, the news that his friend Rufius had been appointed Praefect of the City. It will be remembered that when Rutilius started from Rome, Rufius was the friend who went with him part of the way to Ostia, after all the others who had been to see him off had turned back. On receiving this news of the honor which had come to his friend, Rutilius was so overjoyed that he almost thought of returning to Rome. This Rufius came of a distinguished family, and it is interesting to notice how many members of this family of Gauls held high office in Rome. The friend of Rutilius was Praefect of Rome, as we see, in the year 416. His father had held the same office in the year 399, his grandfather in 365, his great-grandfather in 335, and his great-great grandfather in the year 310. Thus these honors in the Rufius family ran through a whole century. Rutilius regretted that he could not give his friend's full name in the poem, but the rules of metric verse prevented this. The full name, which is learned from other sources, was Ceionius Rufius Volusianus, and since the last name has three short syllables in succession, it could not be used in elegiac verse. Perhaps it is just as well that the rules of metre did prevent the use of the full name in the poem, for it does not seem as if Ceionius Rufius Volusianus could have a really melodious sound in any kind of verse.

After passing the night in the vicinity of Populonia they made another early start on the morning of the fifth day. As they sailed along they had a distant view of the mountains of Corsica, and Rutilius tells a curious local tradition about the discovery of the island. The story was that a herdswoman noticed that one of the cows used to swim away from the shore occasionally, and after remaining away for some time it would return fatter and in better condition than it had been before. The herdswoman reported this, search was made and a fertile island was discovered. The name of the woman was Corsa, and so the name Corsica was given to the island in her honor. Since the distance between the island and the mainland is about fifty miles, it would seem that that cow must have been a champion swimmer as well as an explorer. They also saw Capraria, a rocky, rather desolate island filled, Rutilius says, with " men who shun the light," that is, with a company of monks, men who want to be alone, as the name implies. The life led by monks, and especially their attitude toward human life, seemed to Rutilius so unnatural as to be positively unhuman. Their desire for solitude he denounced as abnormal and their asceticism and the privations which they imposed on themselves he ridiculed. Rutilius felt very strongly on that subject. To him the whole idea of monasticism was revolting, as it was to many other educated Pagans of his time. Nor was this feeling confined

to Pagans alone. There were many Christians also to whom the
theory was as incomprehensible as it was to Pagans. Ausonius
for instance, an older contemporary of Rutilius, was a Christian,
but he was both shocked and deeply grieved when a favorite young
pupil of his suddenly left Bordeaux, went off to a self-imposed
exile in Spain, and became a monk. It is said that the ruins of the
monastery to which Rutilius refers in the island of Capraria may
still be seen there.

The next stopping place was Volaterra Vada where the approach
to the shore was very difficult because of sandbanks. Rutilius
describes the skilful steering and says that the sandbanks, while
they made the place difficult of access, afforded shelter from rough
seas to ships that were small enough to enter the channel. He
does not however say anything of the town, and that may indicate
that the town had ceased to exist even before his time. All we
know of it now is that there had once been a town which is mentioned by both Cicero and Pliny, the site of which is probably
marked by an ancient tower called the Torre di Vada. During
his stay in this vicinity Rutilius was entertained at the villa of a
friend. Soon after they landed one of those torrential rains came
which are well known in Italy, such a fierce rain, he says, that
they could hardly endure it even in the house. Rutilius always
likes to talk about his friends and he tells us something of this
Albinus whose guest he was and who had been his successor as
Praefect of Rome. Then he describes a visit to some salt-works
not far away in which he was much interested. These salt-works
are mentioned in other writings more than three hundred years
after Rutilius wrote of them, but they have now entirely disappeared. Because of bad weather the party was detained here at
the villa of Albinus longer than they had intended to stay, but the
unexpected arrival of another friend made Rutilius very glad of
the delay. This friend, Victorinus, was another Gaul and a native
of Toulouse. He had been obliged to leave Toulouse when that
city was taken by the Visigoths in the year 413, and although he
might have returned afterwards, he preferred to stay on in
Etruria. Rutilius speaks of him in very high terms, telling of his
success as governor of Britain, but says that he declined other
public offices because of his love of country life. Rutilius says
also that in seeing Victorinus he seemed to be enjoying his own

patria. Since this word *patria* was very commonly used in the time of the Empire to denote the home town, it is very probable that it is so used here. If so, it makes it certain that Toulouse was the native town of Rutilius, or that his home was near that city. What he has said in the introduction to the poem implies a country estate rather than a city home.

On the sixth day of the journey they start very early in the morning again and pass the island of Gorgon, now called Gorgona, a barren island about twenty miles from Livorno. This island now has few inhabitants except fishermen, but it was for a long time occupied by monks. Gorgona had painful associations for Rutilius, because one of his own fellow-citizens, a young man whom he knew personally, had forsaken his home and his family, "by madness driven," and had gone a voluntary exile to this desolate island to live in squalor. Rutilius had no patience with the theory that a man becomes a better man by shunning his fellow-men and living as a recluse. This unhappy youth, he says, actually believed that the divine element in man is fostered by a life of squalor, and how repugnant that idea was to Rutilius we have already seen by what he says of the monks at Capraria. In this passage he goes on to say of the ascetic idea that the theory was a worse poison than Circe's drugs, for it was the bodies of men that she changed and degraded, but monkish asceticism debased their minds. Commentators have used much ingenuity in trying to determine who this young man was, but as these conjectures are all pure guess work, they are of no special interest.

The landing place on the sixth day was at Villa Triturrita, near the Portus Pisanus. Just where the Portus Pisanus was is uncertain, but probably somewhere between Livorno and the mouth of the Arno. The villa, so called, is thought to have been a kind of fortress for the protection of the harbor. The remarkable character of the Portus Pisanus is discussed. Although it lay open to the sea and the winds, yet it was a safe refuge for ships because it was protected by a barrier of floating sea-weed. This sea-weed did no harm to ships when it collided with them, but there was such a quantity of it and it was so closely tangled that it checked the waves as they rolled in from the open sea. The next morning the wind was favorable for sailing, but Rutilius wanted to drive to Pisa to see an old friend. This was another

eminent Gaul, Protadius by name, and of him much may be
learned from other sources as well as from what Rutilius says.
Rutilius would doubtless have gone to Pisa to visit this friend in
any case, but he was also especially interested in going there because his father had once been governor of Tuscany and had
lived in Pisa. The pleasure which Rutilius felt in seeing this city
is very evident. He speaks of the cordial welcome which he received from the old men who had known his father personally,
and of his gratification in learning that his father's memory was
still venerated in Tuscany. He also had the pleasure of seeing a
statue of his father which the people of Pisa had erected in his
honor. Altogether this visit seems to have been most satisfactory. But although Rutilius describes the location of Pisa and
refers to the traditional story of its remote origin, he does not tell
so much about the city as he saw it as we should like to know.
His account however although it really tells very little does give
the impression that Pisa, which in the time of Augustus, according to Strabo, was " not without repute," was still a thriving city
in the early fifth century.

When they returned to the port and were ready to sail, a violent
storm came up suddenly and the sailing was deferred. The sea
continued to be so rough that they delayed sailing for several
days, and one thing that they enjoyed during this stay on land
was a hunting excursion in the woods, for which the inn-keeper
furnished the necessary equipment. At this point in the poem
Rutilius indulges in a poetic description of the storm, and with
this the first book closes. There are only six hundred and forty-
four verses in it and the author apologizes for making the book
so short, but gives as his reason for doing so that most readers
find a small book more convenient than one that is large and
heavy.

In the beginning of the second book Rutilius describes the
beauty of the morning when they start on the seventh day's voyage, and after that there are two long digressions. The first of
these is a description of Italy, inspired evidently by his great love
of Italy and his sorrow in thinking that he will soon be beyond
the border. Referring to the mountain ranges he says that Nature
feared the envy that other nations would feel toward Italy because of its richness and fertility, and therefore the Alps were

made on purpose to be a protection on the north, and the Apen-
nines which slope to the Mediterranean on the one side and to the
Adriatic on the other, were added to be another barrier. This
must have been by design, he says, " if we believe that the uni-
verse was created in accordance with a definite plan, and this
great fabric of the world was by God designed."

From the description of Italy the author passes to an invective
against Stilicho. The change of subject seems abrupt, although
the transition is brought about by the author's opinion that the
very fact that Italy is what it is made Stilicho's crime all the
greater. While many of the individuals mentioned by Rutilius
are so vividly presented that the reader begins to feel acquainted
with them, Stilicho is the only one who is really well known to
history. This son of a Vandal chief who was a general in the
Roman army was practically the ruler of the Empire in the time
of the Emperor Honorius, until he was killed eight years before
this poem was written. Stilicho's somewhat romantic career is
interesting in itself and it is of special interest because of the
violently conflicting opinions that were held of him by his contemporaries. Rutilius makes a very bitter attack on him, accus-
ing him of treachery to the Empire, of betraying Rome to the
barbarians, and of burning the Sibylline Books. The poet
Claudian on the other hand praises Stilicho to the skies, and both
Claudian and Rutilius are undoubtedly representative of many
of their contemporaries. Among modern scholars the difference
of opinion in regard to Stilicho has been quite as great, if not as
violent, as it was in his own time, and it is safe to say that Stilicho
is one of the characters of history in regard to whom posterity will
never agree.

After these two digressions Rutilius returns to the account of
the journey and says that they went on as far as " the shining
walls of Luna." Of this old Etruscan town practically nothing
is known except that it was situated on or near the Gulf of Spezia,
as it is now called, and that it was famous both for its harbor and
for its marble. The marble, now called Carrara marble, has been
famous since the time of Julius Caesar, and Rutilius says of it
that in color " it rivals the fresh-fallen snow." At this point, the
sixty-eighth verse of the second book, the story breaks off, for
the remainder of the book is lost. And here by the Gulf of Spezia

while he is admiring the beauty of Carrara marble, we have to
take an abrupt leave of Rutilius, for nothing more is known of
him. Whether he ever went back to Rome or not, whether he ever
reached home or not, whether the poem was ever finished or not,
these are questions that must remain forever unanswered.
We have seen that the time spent on the boats in going from
Ostia to the Gulf of Spezia was seven days, or rather parts of
seven days, for they always passed the night on shore, generally
landed early enough to take some excursion before dark, and in
one case at least they landed at noon. But although there were
only seven days when they were on board ship for even a part of
the day, the time spent on the journey was over six weeks, from
October 7 when they left Ostia to November 22 when they arrived at Luna. The journey was certainly made in a very leisurely
way, even though some of the delays were caused by bad weather.
Although Rutilius felt it his duty to return home to his estate in
Gaul, he seems to have been in no great hurry to arrive. There
is nothing strange in that however, for after the number of years
that he had been away the difference of a few weeks in the time
of his arrival would not be a matter of any great importance.
For himself on the other hand it was of importance to make the
most of the journey. He evidently wanted to see all that he
could on the way. It is the journey of a tourist that is described,
or rather of a small party for Rutilius was not travelling alone,
and after seeing how modern tourist parties are whizzed through
Italy, it is refreshing to read the itinerary of a journey which was
so free from hurry.

This poem of Rutilius consists of two distinct parts each of
which is complete without the other, the account of the journey
and the panegyric on Rome. But although each is complete without the other, neither can be said to be independent of the other,
for the combination of the two gives an additional interest to both.
The account of the journey would be far less vivid and less interesting if we did not know the reason for taking it, if we had not
begun to feel acquainted with the author before he started and
to sympathize with his sorrow at leaving Rome. The panegyric
on Rome might indeed have been written at any time, anywhere,
under any circumstances, but the fact that it was written just
when it was, under stress of deep emotion, that it was such an

outburst of enthusiasm, such a spontaneous expression of his love and admiration for Rome called forth by his sorrow at going away, this gives an added force to all that he says. It is probable that this panegyric was written during the stay at Ostia just before he sailed, while he could still look toward Rome and fancy that he saw the seven hills which he so loved. He writes as if Rome were actually in sight from Ostia, and although that is not the case, the view of Rome was just as clearly before his mind as if he were seeing it with his eyes.

The panegyric is in the form of a direct address to Rome and the main outline of it may be given briefly, together with the translation of a few verses here and there. It begins

> Hear, fairest Queen of all the world,
> Mother of men and mother of the gods,
> Not far from heaven through thy temples
> Do we dwell.
> Of thee we sing and always will
> So long as fate allows.
> No one can forget thee while he
> Lives and breathes.
> Sooner shall oblivion crush down the sun
> Than honor for thee shall pass from our hearts.

Then he refers to the vastness of the Empire, how it extends from the rising to the setting sun, and of how Rome throughout that vast domain had inspired loyalty, going on to say,

> Thou hast given one fatherland
> To nations widely scattered,
> For to the conquered thou didst give
> A share in thy own laws,
> And thou hast made a city
> Of what was once the world.

After speaking of how Rome is honored in every part of the Empire, he refers to some of the earlier empires and to the fact that no one of them could compare with that of Rome. And yet, he says, Rome's strength originally was no greater than that of those earlier powers. It was not in military success that she surpassed them. It was not force, but the wisdom and justice of her rule that made it enduring. Rome's success was due not so much to

her ability to conquer, but rather to her genius in making friends
of the conquered.

> That thou dost reign is a lesser thing
> Than that thou dost deserve to reign;
> The greatness of thy destiny thou hast surpassed
> By the greatness of thy deeds.

To enumerate the whole list of Rome's victories, he says, would
be like trying to count the stars. Then he goes on to speak of the
City as he saw it, of the glittering temples, of the aqueducts
where intercepted rivers are stored, of the great bathing establishments which consume whole lakes. He refers to the dashing spray
of the fountains, not unlike those in which Rome still rejoices, to
the abundance of pure drinking water, in which Rome still takes
justifiable pride, and to the numerous parks with their birds and
their colonnades. He refers also to those wonderful spring days
which sometimes come in winter months and are so familiar to
all who have ever lived in Rome, and, equally familiar to those
who know Rome, to that cool breeze which tempers summer's
heat. Then Rome is exhorted never to lose courage.

> " Rear high thy laurelled locks, renew, Oh Rome,
> Youth's vernal tresses on thy reverend brow."
> Let the disaster thou hast suffered be forgotten,
> Let thy contempt for suffering heal thy wounds.

It has always been Rome's custom, he says, in adversity to hope
for prosperity. He enumerates several of the enemies with whom
Rome had contended in her long history of over a thousand years,
and while she had suffered much and many times, she had never
despaired. As it has been so it shall be, Rutilius firmly believes,
and Rome is exhorted to go on and spread civilization throughout
the Roman centuries. Rome's years to come, he says, shall have
no limit " while earth endures, while heaven still bears the stars."
Then follows a prayer for prosperity throughout the Empire, and
the panegyric closes with the wish, he hardly dares to call it hope,
but with the wish that, whether he ever returns to Rome or not,
Rome might remember him.

There are several points in this panegyric which are to be especially noticed. The first, and perhaps the most important, is

that Rutilius in the fifth century had just as great confidence in Rome and in Rome's future as any poet of the Augustan Age had had. There were two other Roman poets in this late period whose confidence in Rome was no less than that of Rutilius, Claudian, a Greek, and Prudentius, a Spaniard. Claudian like Rutilius was a Pagan, while Prudentius was a Christian, but they were all three alike in their belief that the hope for the future of civilization lay in the mission of Rome. And it was not simply their own belief that these poets expressed, but a belief that was very prevalent in the age in which they lived. They were quite right too, these men of the late Empire, in believing that Rome's mission had not been finished, even though the Empire was crumbling and Rome was gradually ceasing to be what it had been. Rome's mission had not been finished in the fifth century, and it has not been finished and it will not be finished in the twentieth. There are some critics who cannot quite forgive Rutilius for having such faith in Rome in this late period. They think that he ought to have realized that the Empire was breaking up, that he ought to have foreseen the dark ages that were to come. But it is hardly fair to criticize him because he did not see his own time in just the light which has been thrown upon it by subsequent history. Moreover if he could have looked forward a few centuries, he could have looked forward a longer period still. If he could have foreseen the Dark Ages, he could have foreseen also the Renaissance and the Italy of the twentieth century. Critics have called Rutilius blind because of his faith in Rome, but now more than fifteen hundred years after the poem was written we may believe perhaps that this faith was due not to blindness, but to vision. The history of Rome and its various vicissitudes all down through the ages is a fascinating story, and there have been times when Rome's future looked dark, but in the third decade of the twentieth century there is no reason for despairing of the future of Rome.

Another point that is very noticeable is that in the panegyric there is nothing said of the invasion of Rome by the Visigoths under Alaric which had occurred only six years before the poem was written. The only allusion to it is in two verses already quoted,

> Let the disaster thou hast suffered be forgotten,
> Let thy contempt for suffering heal thy wounds,

and these do not of themselves imply any exceptional or very recent disaster. The fact that nothing is said of this invasion is of special interest because the accounts of it which have come down to us are conflicting. It was in the year 410 that the Visigoths entered Rome. Rutilius, as we have seen, was Praefect of the City in 414, and in the year 412 he held the office of *Magister Officiorum*. Just how long he had been living in Rome before that we do not know, but it must have been for a considerable time, for this office which was called *Magister Officiorum* was one of the most important and most responsible in the whole civil administration. It is inconceivable that a stranger in the city should have been appointed to such an office as that. It is therefore not only possible but very probable that Rutilius was in Rome at the time of the invasion. In any case if the destruction in the city had been as great as it is represented in some of the accounts, he could not have ignored it in writing of Rome. The fact that he does ignore it serves therefore to confirm the theory that in some of the accounts the disaster was exaggerated. While it is not possible to determine just how much damage was done to the city at that time, there are certain things which it is possible to learn. First, the most terrible accounts were written by people who were far away from Rome, and who relied to some extent on rumor and to some extent on their own imaginations as to what the disaster must have been. Second, the attack of the Visigoths was a blockade rather than a siege. It was by famine rather than force that the city was taken. Third, the Visigoths were in the city only a few days, and they cared much more for plunder than for destruction. For that reason, while a great quantity of valuables and portable property of various kinds was carried away, the destruction in the city was much less than it would otherwise have been. The fact that the worst accounts are undoubtedly exaggerated, is of course no reason for trying to minimize the disaster, but in any case whatever damage was done, it is certain that the recovery was very rapid, both the material recovery and the recovery of morale.